ASAO Special Publications No. 1

Historical Metaphors and Mythical Realities

Structure in the Early History of the Sandwich Islands Kingdom

Marshall Sahlins

THE UNIVERSITY OF MICHIGAN PRESS
Ann Arbor

Library of Congress Cataloging in Publication Data

Sahlins, Marshall David, 1930–
    Historical metaphors and mythical realities.

    (ASAO special publications ; no. 1)
    Bibliography: p.
    1. Hawaiians—Social life and customs.
2. Hawaiians—Religion. 3. Acculturation—Hawaii.
4. Hawaii—Discovery and exploration—English.
5. Cook, James, 1728–1779. 6. Structural
anthropology. I. Title. II. Series: Association
for Social Anthropology in Oceania. ASAO special
publications ; no. 1.
GN671.H3S23   996.9   80–28649
ISBN 0–472–02721–2 (pbk.)

Historical Metaphors
and
Mythical Realities

*My book is devoted to exploring the history of
a structure and the structure of a history—*

Paul Friedrich, *Aphrodite,* 1978

*It is not the structuralists who put the structures
in history—*

Jean Pouillon, *Les Temps Modernes,* 1966

Preface

This monograph is a way of looking culturally at a certain history. The introductory and concluding chapters discuss the theoretical perspective briefly, but for the most part the general ideas on history are interwoven with the concrete happenings that demonstrate them. The history at issue is an exotic one, having to do with the reaction of indigenous Hawaiian culture to circumstances posed by the appearance of Captain Cook and later European explorers, traders and missionaries. It might thus seem that the theoretical explication of the historical occurrences has an equally limited relevance, that it is pertinent (at best) to this and similar episodes of "acculturation." My argument, however, runs on the opposed assumption—which in the end must be judged from the results: that such a confrontation of cultures affords a privileged occasion for seeing very common types of historical change *en clair*. The general statements I derive about historical processes do not require conditions of intercultural contact. They suppose only a world on which people act differentially and according to their respective situations as social beings, conditions that are as common to action within a given society as they are to the interaction of distinct societies. My history cannot claim to be Marxist, but it has the same minimum and sufficient premises: that men and women are suffering beings because they act at once in relationship to each other and in a world that has its own relationships.

The present work constitutes a stage in a larger project of research and publication. It originated in, and is expanded from, the honorary lecture of similar title delivered at the annual meeting of the Association for Social Anthropology in Oceania, Clearwater, Florida, 23 February 1979. It will eventuate in a still wider study, to be called: *The Dying God or the*

History of the Sandwich Islands as Culture. The first volume (of a projected three) is in preparation, and will provide documentation beyond what has seemed necessary here.

I am grateful to Michael Silverstein for giving the final manuscript the benefit of his fine critical eye. And to Dorothy Barrère and Valerio Valeri for the collaboration and conversation which have been indispensable to my grasp of things Hawaiian. Of course I am solely responsible for the deficiencies in this knowledge, but my main creative responsibility in the present monograph has consisted in historically contextualizing it. Finally, gratitude to Susan Martich for once more turning an illegible handwriting into a perfect typescript.

The research was funded by National Science Research Foundation Grant GS-28718x and by the Lichtstern Fund, Department of Anthropology, University of Chicago.

Contents

Hānaipū Ceremony at the "House of Lono," Kealakekua, Hawaii, 19 January 1779, (John Webber).

The Death of Cook (John Webber), 14 February 1779, at Ka'awaloa, Kealakekua, Hawaii.

1 Introduction
History and Structural Theory

SYNCHRONY/DIACHRONY AND LANGUE/PAROLE

Structural anthropology was founded in a binary opposition, of the kind that would later become its trademark: a radical opposition to history. Working from Saussure's model of language as a scientific object, structuralism similarly privileged system over event and synchrony over diachrony. In a way parallel to the Saussurean distinction between language *(la langue)* and speech *(la parole),* structural analysis seemed also to exclude individual action and worldly practice, except as they represented the projection or "execution" of the system in place (cf. Bourdieu 1977). I will argue here, mainly by concrete demonstration, that all these scruples are not really necessary, that one can determine structures in history—and vice versa.

For Saussure (1966 [1915]) the disengagement of structure from history had seemed requisite, inasmuch as language could be systematically analyzed only as it was autonomous, referentially arbitrary and a collective phenomenon. Saussure's notion of "system" was indeed like a Kantian category of "community." Community is founded on a temporally discrete judgment, as of a whole having many parts, which are thus comprehended as mutually determining: "as coordinated with, not subordinated to each other, and so as determining each other, not in one direction only, as in a series, but reciprocally, as in an aggregate—if one member of the division [into parts] is posited, all the rest are excluded, and conversely" (Kant 1965:117). Any given element in such a community, say one of several distinguishable objects in a landscape, is comprehended as such by its existing relationships with the others: as a differential or positional value, conditioned by the presence

3

of the others. The parts being thus constituted by reciprocal, contemporaneous relationships, time is ruled out of the intelligibility.

So it is, Saussure held, with language. The conceptual value of the sign is fixed by relationships with co-existing signs. By its contrasts with the other signs of its (systemic) environment, its own sense or conceptual value is sedimented. The value of "green" is determined by the presence alongside it of "blue," and vice versa. If, as is true in many natural languages, there were no "blue," then "green" would have greater conceptual and referential extension. Hence language can be analyzed as a structure only insofar as it is considered as a *state,* its elements standing in the temporal order of simultaneity.

Moreover, it would be as futile to search for the system in history as it would be to introduce history into the system. Invoking the independence of sound shifts by relation to sign values, Saussure's arguments to this effect appear as a classic distinction between physical contents and formal relationships. Contents (sounds) change independently of relationships (which determine values). In this perspective—now better understood as the "duality of patterning" feature of language—phonetic shifts had seemed but physical happenstance, by contrast to the systematic mental processes at the level of sign relationships. Arising in speech, phonetic shifts are thus considered by Saussure "independent events," accidental from the vantage point of structure. They have to do simply with sequences of sound, without regard to the meaningful values of the lexical and grammatical units they inhabit. Values, on the other hand, depend solely on concurrent relationships between the terms of language, without regard to their phonetic contents (so long as sufficient contrast in sound is maintained to allow for the differentiation of meaning). Alterations in sound are thus encompassed in the grammar of relationships, or even extended analogically (i.e., on systemic principles), to the extent that there is no "inner bond" or adequate relation between the change in sound and the linguistic effects that ensue. Hence the fatal argument that was to be picked up by a structural anthropology: from the perspective of a system of signs, the changes to which it submits will appear fortuitous. The only *system* consists in the way these historical materials are interrelated at any given time or state of the language.

But if this language is indeed systematic and analyzable as such, its signs must also be arbitrary. As it were, language is a meaningful system in and for itself: its signs determined as values purely by reciprocal relationships with other signs, as distinct from any connection with the objects to which they may refer. For if a sign had some necessary or inherent link to its referent, its value would not result solely from relationships to other signs. The notion of language as an autonomous structure is then compromised. It loses coherence or systematicity, inasmuch as certain values are externally imposed and carry over through time regardless of contemporaneous relationships within the language. In at least certain types of social practice, Saussure believed, signs do take on just such necessary relationships to their referents. Economics, for example. According to Saussure, the value of "land" as an economic category depends to some extent on the inherent productivity of land. But then, to that extent the value is not a differential function in and of a system of signs; rather, "land" here has subsisting conceptual content or meaning. We can thus have history, value in a temporal mode, but at the expense of system.

STRUCTURE VS. *PRAXIS* IN HISTORIC TIME

Saussure foresaw the advent of a general "semiology" that would be concerned with the role of signs in social life. Yet it would seem by his view that values in such domains as economics, since they are "somehow rooted in things," cannot be treated as purely semiotic, thus susceptible to the same kind of analysis as language—even though it also seems that the constituent elements of these cultural domains are indeed sign values. A similar dilemma is posed to a general semiology, a cultural structuralism, by the distinction between language and speech. Speech likewise presents the sign in the form of a "heterogeneous" object, subject to other considerations than the pure relationships among signs. For the expression of language in speech is notoriously imperfect and endlessly variable, conditioned by all sorts of biographical accidents of the speaker. This is once more to say that the determination of discourse goes quite beyond the relationships between the terms of a linguistic system, to facts of a different nature: sociological, psychological, even physiological. Hence the necessity, for Saussure, of constituting language in its collective dimension, apart from its individual implementations in discourse. It exists as a perfect semiotic system only in the community of speakers.

Yet consider what is then excluded from a meaningful *cum* structural analysis. In speech is History made. Here signs are set in various and contingent relationships according to people's instrumental purposes—purposes of course that are socially constituted even as they may be individually variable. Signs thus take on functional and implicational values in a project of action, not merely the mutual determinations of a synchronic state. They are subjected to analysis and recombination, from which arise unprecedented forms and meanings (metaphors, for example). Above all, in speech people bring signs into indexical relationships with the objects of their projects, as these objects form the perceived context for speech as a social activity. Such a context is indeed a signified context; the meanings of its objects may even by presupposed by the act of discourse. On the other hand, the world may not conform to the presuppositions by which some people talk about it. In the event, speech brings signs into "new" contexts of use, entailing contradictions which must be in turn encompassed by the system. Value is truly constituted in a system of signs, but people use and experience signs as the names of things, hence they condition and potentially revise the general conceptual values of linguistic terms and relations by reference to a world. The encounter with the word is itself a valuation, and a potential revaluation, of signs.

If structural/semiotic analysis is to be extended to general anthropology on the model of its pertinence to "language," then what is lost is not merely history and change, but practice—human action in the world. Some might think that what is lost is what anthropology is all about. For them, the prospect is enough to reject such structuralism out of hand. On the other hand, it is possible that the sacrifices apparently attending structural analysis—history, event, action, the world—are not truly required. Structural linguistics went on from Saussure to transcend the opposition of history and system, at least in certain respects. Jakobson (1961:16–23, 202–220) would argue that even sound shifts are systematic, insofar as they are comprehended by a "phonemic system," and their analysis requires working back and forth between synchrony and diachrony. At the same time, anthropology was learning that the value of any cultural category whatever, such as "land," is indeed arbitrary in the sense that it is constituted on principled distinctions among signs which, in relation to objects, are never the only possible distinctions. Even an ecological anthropology would recognize that the extent to which a particular tract of land is a "productive resource," if it is at all, depends on the cultural order in place. Economics might thus find a place in the general semiology that Saussure envisioned—while at the same time hedging the entrance requirements with restrictive clauses.

Despite all this, structuralism was originally brought over into general anthropology with its theoretical limitations intact. It seemed that history had to be kept at a distance, lest "system" be put at risk. As I say, action entered into account only as it represented the working out of an established order, the "stereotypic reproduction" (Godelier's phrase) of existing cultural categories. This nonhistorical appropriation of action could be supported, moreover, by the sound argument that circumstances have no existence or effect in culture except as they are interpreted. And interpretation is, after all, classification within a given category. "It is not enough to say," the philosopher tells us, "that one is conscious *of* something; one is also conscious of something as *being something"* (Percy 1958:638, emphases added). The percept becomes a fact of human consciousness—or at least of social communication—insofar as it is embedded in a concept of which the perceiver is not the author. The concept is motivated in the culture as constituted. When Captain Cook sailed into Kealakekua Bay, Hawaii, on 17 January 1779, the Hawaiians did not take it all for what it "really" was. " 'Now our bones shall live,' " they are reputed to have said, " 'our *'aumakua* [ancestral spirit] has returned' " (Kamakau 1961:98). Or, if this tradition be doubted, there is no doubt from contemporary records that such was how the Hawaiians ritually received the famous navigator. The event thus enters culture as an instance of a received category, the worldly token of a presupposed type. It would seem to follow that the pertinent theory of culture and history is *plus ça change.* . . .

I argue in succeeding chapters that, to adopt Jean Pouillon's *bon mot,* the theory is better reversed: *plus c'est la même chose, plus ça change* (Pouillon 1977). When Captain Cook was killed at Kealakekua Bay, this victory became a novel source of the legitimacy of Hawaiian kings for decades afterwards. Through the appropriation of Cook's bones, the *mana* of the Hawaiian kingship itself became British. And long after the English as men had lost their godliness, the Hawaiian gods kept their Englishness. Moreover, the effect was to give the British a political presence in Hawaiian affairs that was all out of proportion to their actual existence in Hawaiian waters, since they were rapidly displaced in the vital provisioning and sandalwood trade by the Americans. For that matter, Cook's divinity was no *sequitur* to the actual force he exerted. More important was the fact that Hawaiians had killed *him.*

Hence, if structuralism seems incapable of giving a theoretical account of historical change, neither do the current utilitarian theories, whether ecological or historical materialist, afford a sufficient alternative. These practical notions of culture would offer us a history on the model of a physics. Symbols are symptoms, direct or mystified, of the true force of things. Culture may set conditions to the historical process, but it is dissolved and reformulated in material practice, so that history becomes the realization, in the form of society, of the actual resources people put into play.

As is well known, German social thought from Dilthey to Weber criticized this historical physics. Indeed, the American concept of culture (and modern structuralism) owes a great deal to German romanticism through the mediation of Boas, Benedict and others. Perhaps the gains in understanding might now be repaid to history. What anthropology could provide in return is the idea that the historical efficacy of persons, objects and events, as in the example of the British in Hawaii, arises in their cultural value. Another word for such value is "significance," a contrastive position in a scheme of relationships, and the term, by its double connotation of 'meaningfulness' and 'importance,' happily summarizes the historical theory. Perhaps it is too much to claim that Maitland's famous dictum should be reversed: that history will be anthropology, or it will be nothing. My object in this essay is more modest, simply to show some ways that history is organized by structures of significance.

To a degree, the task is not difficult, since the ready structuralist notion of *plus ça change* . . .is a very historical idea. The past, it says, is always with us. From a structuralist perspective nothing is simpler than the discovery of continuities of cultural categories as modes of interpretation and action: the celebrated "structures of the *longue durée*" (Braudel 1958). I shall begin discussion of the Hawaiian kingdom with considerations of this kind. But only to lay the groundwork for a more ambitious project. The great challenge to an historical anthropology is not merely to know how events are ordered by culture, but how, in that process, the culture is reordered. How does the reproduction of a structure become its transformation?

[handwritten annotations:]

α Significance of history arises in their cultural value

Continuities of cultural categories — of Hawaiian kingdom

How events are ordered by culture, but how, in that process, the culture is reordered.

not [events are ordered by culture] — but how the culture is reordered

2 Reproduction

Structures of the Long Run

GODS FROM KAHIKI

There is a story often repeated in European annals of the strenuous efforts made by Vancouver—or in one version, by a certain "Padre" Howell—to convince the Hawaiian King Kamehameha of the comparative merits of Christianity. The date would have been 1793 or 1794. In 1798, the American trader Townsend heard that,

> Capt. Vancouver was very anxious to Christianize these people, but that can never be done until they are more civilized. The King Amma-amma-hah [Kamehameha] told Capt. Vancouver that he would go with him to the high mountain Mona Roah [Mauna Loa] and they would both jump off together, each calling on their separate gods for protection, and if Capt, Vancouver's god saved him, but himself was not saved by his god, then his people should believe as Capt. Vancouver did. (Townsend 1888:74; cf. Cleveland n.d.: 211)

The Russian Golovnin added, in 1818:

> This experiment did not appeal to Vancouver, and he not only declined to perform it, he did not even mention it in his *Voyage*. Thus ended the discussion on religion. (Golovnin 1979:207)

Hawaiian history often repeats itself, since only the second time is it an event. The first time it is myth. Kamehameha's proposition to Vancouver was actually a legendary allusion. The suggestion was that they reenact the story of the celebrated Paao[1] who many generations earlier had

9

come, like Vancouver, from invisible lands beyond the horizon to institute a new religion—indeed, to install along with his religion a new line of ruling chiefs, from whom Kamehameha traced his own descent. As the myth goes:

> It was said that many gods asked Paao to accept and worship them as his deities. He had built his house on the edge of a precipice from which the *koa'e* (Bos'n bird) flew. Whenever any gods came to him, Paao told them to fly from that precipice. The one returning alive should be his god and receive his worship. But when they leaped from the cliff they were dashed to pieces at its base. [To abbreviate: such was the fate of the would-be gods Lelekoae and Makuapali, but Makuakaumana flew into Paao's canoe and became his god.] (Kamakau *in* Thrum 1923:46–47)

The Vancouver story may well be apocryphal.[2] But if it is not a fact of Hawaiian history, it is its truth—its "poetic logic." The story succinctly encodes the entire Hawaiian theory of the European presence, notably of Vancouver's predecessor, Captain Cook. Indeed, in certain late versions of the Paao myth, the priest himself is said to have been a white man (Ellis 1828:398; Byron 1826:4). The Europeans were to the Hawaiians in general as the latter's own chiefs—likewise godlike beings from the invisible lands (Kahiki)—were to the underlying people, upon whom the chiefs violently imposed themselves. "A chief," as the proverb runs, "is a shark that travels on land" (Handy and Pukui 1972:199; cf. Fornander 1916–1919 V. VI:368–410). The allusion is particularly to the disposition of these immigrant chiefs to indulge in human sacrifices (cf. Valeri n.d.).

The legend of Paao is perhaps the most important charter for the advent of the usurping chiefs and the institution of the sacrificial cult. As the story goes:

> Paao was forced to quit his original homeland because of a quarrel with his older brother, Lonopele, a famous farmer. When Lonopele accused Paao's son of stealing some fruit, Paao opened the boy's stomach only to find he had been innocent. Enraged, Paao determined to leave his brother and had a canoe constructed for that purpose. By a ruse, Lonopele's own son was entrapped into a transgression of the canoe-building tabus, allowing Paao to offer him as the human sacrifice that would complete the work. Paao then sailed off with a number of men and (in certain versions) the feather god, Kukailimoku (Ku-snatcher-of-the-island). Lonopele raised a series of storms of the "Kona" type (a winter storm) to destroy the canoe, but Paao successfully invoked schools of bonito *(aku)* and mackerel *(opelu)* fish to calm the sea. Weathering other dangers sent by Lonopele, Paao finally reached Hawaii Island, where he constructed certain famous temples. These were the first temples of human sacrifice, the rites presided over by the god Ku (of which Paao's feather god is an important form). In one version (Kepelino 1932:58), Paao also slaughtered all the pre-existing priests. The political changes he simultaneously introduced are variously recounted. Either Hawaii was at that time without a chief, or it was being governed badly by the existing chief (sometimes identified as Kapawa). In the latter case, Paao deposed the chief, and by all accounts he installed a new ruler brought from Kahiki, Pilikaaiea. The Hawaii Island rulers trace to

this chief (about 20 generations before Kamehameha). Apart from the temple form, human sacrificial rites and the feather god Kukailimoku, Paao is also said to have brought image worship to Hawaii, as well as certain sacred insignia of the chieftainship and the prostration tabu accorded divine chiefs. (Kamakau 1865, ms.; Thrum 1923:46–52; Kepelino 1932:20, 58; Westervelt 1923:65–78; Malo 1951:6–7; Remy 1861:3–4; Fornander 1969 v.2:33–40)

The myth is fundamental. Without attempting an extensive analysis or comparisons between variants, I shall underline a few allusions pertinent to the present discussion.

Kukailimoku is the personal conqueror-god of famous Hawaii Island rulers, notably Kamehameha and his predecessor of Cook's time, Kalaniopuu. Kapawa (a.k.a. Heleipawa), the ruler deposed by Paao, represents a chief and cult of another sort. By tradition, Kapawa was the first Hawaiian chief born and installed at the inland temple of Kukaniloko on Oahu. The area, the temple and the installation rites signify an earlier, more indigenous type of ruling chief: succeeding by inherent right and tabu status rather than by usurpation; benevolent to his people; sponsor of agricultural production and provider of other wealth; and, above all, the chief who eschews human sacrifice (Kamakau *in* Thrum 1923:85–93).

The reference to Kona storms along with the bonito and the mackerel invokes the same theory of usurpation, but is set and enacted in a different code, the annual ritual alternation of the gods Lono and Ku. The transition from mackerel to bonito fishing marks the definitive end of ceremonies celebrating the sojourn in the Islands of the peaceable and productive god Lono. Come with the winter rains to renew the fertility of nature and the gardens of the people, Lono's advent is the occasion of an elaborate and prolonged rite of four lunar months called the Makahiki (Year). During this period the normal Ku ceremonies, including human sacrifice, are suspended. At the end of the Makahiki, however, Lono returns to the invisible land (Kahiki—or to the sky, which is the same) whence he had come. Ku, together with his earthly representative, the ruling chief, now regains the ascendancy.[3] The historic significance of all this is that Captain Cook was by Hawaiian conceptions a form of Lono; whereas the chief with whom he dealt and who would ritually claim his death, Kalaniopuu—he was Ku (on the Makahiki, see Malo 1951; Kamakau *in* Fornander 1916–1919, v.6:34ff; Valeri: n.d.).

The incidents of Cook's life and death at Hawaii were in many respects historical metaphors of a mythical reality. Nor was Cook the only legendary figure Hawaiians identified as Lono. He had several predecessors in the genealogies of ruling chiefs: Laamaikahiki (Consecrated-One-from-Kahiki, whose story must be read with that of his father Moikeha), Lonoikamakahiki (Lono-of-the-Makahiki), and Kalaninuiimamao, father of the ruling chief of Cook's time (cf. Beckwith 1972). Their legends have a common denominator—amounting to another representation of the theory of political and seasonal succession. As it concerns the loss of the sacred chiefess, thus rank and reproductive power at the same time, this code mediates beautifully between the political and cosmological dimensions of the theory.

The chiefly figurations of Lono, predecessors of Cook in this role, were all descendants of women of relatively indigenous or early lines. They were likewise married to sacred women, but all lost their wives and chiefdoms to upstart rulers. Hence like the Makahiki god Lono, theirs was the original power over the fertility of the land. The indispensability of this native reproductive power is attested as much in the customary practice of usurping chiefs as in the categories of myth or rite. For usurpation is typically marked, either as means or consequence, by the appropriation of the ranking woman of the deposed line: to produce a child not only tabu by mother-right but, as descendent at once of the usurper and the usurped, a child that synthesizes the contrasting qualities of rule, mana and tabu, in the highest form. So did Kamahemeha marry the daughter (Keopuolani) of his deposed predecessor (Kiwalao), to sire by her his heir (Liholiho). Kamehameha, moreover, desired that his successor be born at the temple of Kukaniloko, temple of the ancient chiefly right, though this project was frustrated by his wife's illness. In the same vein, Hawaiian tradition has it that Captain Cook, on first coming to Kauai, was offered and took the firstborn daughter of the ranking Kauai chiefess (Remy 1861:18). The story is again inaccurate, yet faithful to Hawaiian categories, and in this respect true evidence of the system in Hawaiian historical action.

Cook in fact was not about to yield to temptations of the flesh, though quite prepared, when there was no danger of introducing "the venereal," to allow his "people" to so make display of their mortal weaknesses. According to Zimmermann, who was on the companion ship *Discovery,* Cook never spoke of religion, would tolerate no priest on his ship, seldom observed the sabbath and never "was there the slightest suspicion of his having intercourse with the women" (Zimmermann 1930:99–100). It appears that there could be only one Authority on board a vessel of His Majesty's Navy. Hence if Hawaiians really did present their sacred chiefess to Captain Cook because he was a god, as local tradition has it, we can be sure that he refused her—for something like the same reason.

I shall return to Cook, Paao, Vancouver and Christianity, but some discussion seems in order of this capacity of Hawaiian culture to reproduce itself as history.

HISTORY AS MYTH, EPIC AND COSMIC TRAVELOGUE

Polynesian cosmology may lend itself in a specially powerful way to stereotypic reproduction. Strong logical continuities link the earliest elements of cosmogonic myths to the chiefly heroes of the latest historical legends. True, the original categories may be abstract conceptions in barely personified form, such as the Maori 'Nothingness,' 'Thought,' 'Observation' and 'Desire'; or, succeeding these, basic constituents of the universe, such as Rangi (Sky [Father]) and Papa (Earth [Mother]). But then, the narrative sequence and interaction of the categorical beings serves as a model, transposable to many different domains, of the right relations between things. The Maori story of Rangi and Papa is a paradigm of spatial values, political relations, the interaction of men and women, and much more. Continuity between such beginnings and the present, between abstract categories and historical persons, is guaranteed by the unbroken succession of births between them. Later heroes are genealogical descendants of generic concepts, and so transpose the relationships of the concepts in an historico-pragmatic mode, i.e., as their own natures and deeds. The heroes of legend and the protagonists of history, down to the *dramatis personae* of everyday existence, are instantiations of cultural classes (Grey 1956; Best 1923, 1924; White 1887–1890; Taylor 1870; Johansen 1954; Smith 1974–1975; Salmond 1978).

Polynesian concepts of descent provide the logical means of this cultural repetition. For descent is a relation of genus to species. Just as the father is to his sons, so the ancestor stands to his descendants as a general class to its specific instances, a "type" to its "tokens." Where descent groups are corporate, as the Maori *iwi* and *hapu,* they are often named from the ancestor, with a prefix signifying descendants: Ngati-Tuwharetoa, (the descendants of Tuwharetoa)—or can we not say, 'the Tuwharetoas'?—is the usual Maori form, and cognate expressions (e.g., *ati*) are widespread in central and eastern Polynesia. But the name still does not sufficiently convey the sense in which living persons are identified with their forebears. I have heard a Fijian elder narate the doings of his ancestral lineage over several generations *in the first person pronoun.* Johansen cites an experience of Percy Smith to exactly the same effect:

"According to our knowledge the reason why the Ngatiwhatua came to Kaipara was a murder committed by the Ngatikahumateika. This tribe murdered my ancestor, Taureka. The tribe lived in *Hokianga.* This country was theirs, this tribe's. My home was Muriwhenua, it was my permanent residence because my ancestor lived there. Later I left Muriwhenua because of this murder. Then I tried to revenge myself, and Hokianga's people were defeated and I took possession of the old country. Because of this battle the whole of Hokianga was finally taken by me right to Maunganui, and I lived in the country because all the people had been killed." All the events described [Johansen comments] took place long before the narrator was born. (1954:36)

Johansen calls this "the kinship I" and gives other examples of its semantic extent, not only into the past but in reference to contemporaries of the group and future generations. " 'You will kill me,' " says the embattled warrior to his enemies, " 'My tribe will kill you and the land will be mine' " (1954:36). One might paraphrase Rimbaud: "I" is the others.

Myth, then, cannot merely be a set of tricks the living play on the dead, as Malinowski thought: a "charter" that justifies the practical arrangements of the present by their ideological projection as a past. The Maori, as Johansen says, "re-lives history." Mythical incidents constitute archetypal situations. The experiences of celebrated mythical protagonists are re-experienced by the living in analogous circumstances. More, the living *become* mythical heroes. Whakatau was the paradigmatic avenger. He who would now avenge himself "puts on Whakatau." The dying die the primordial death of Maui, who failed in an heroic attempt to conquer death; the mourners thereupon sing the lament of Apakura, whose son was the prototypical sacrificial victim. It is not exactly that the living are "like" the ancients, or even that they "repeat" the latter's deeds and words: "We are so apt to insert in thought a 'like' and in this way make all of it very simple according to our presuppositions. We find it quite obvious that when an event has happened, it never returns; but this is exactly what happens" (Johansen 1954:101).

I refer particularly to the Maori for the contrasts as well as the similarities to Hawaiians. The relation between Maori cosmology and the Hawaiian is something like the distinction between cosmic myth and historical epic that Dumézil found between the Indian tradition and the Roman (e.g., Dumézil 1949:179–17; 1970:60ff.). The Indians, Dumézil observes, think cosmically, philosophically and morally, where the Romans think nationally, practically and politically. Vedic traditions are thus fabulous and mythical, Roman traditions historical: what appear in the former as miraculous deeds of divine beings are in the latter worldly acts of legendary kings. Not that the common Indo-European heritage is lost in the transformation. Rather, the same cultural categories and relationships that are abstractly signified in Indian myth are reproduced in humanized form by the Roman historical epics. The Hawaiian "humanized mythology" contrasts, at least relatively, with Maori cosmology in the same way.

Maori relate a dramatic origin tale of the initial union of Heavens (Rangi) and Earth (Papa), from which coupling of elemental male and female spaces arose the gods that separated them. At a later stage, a god (Tane) generated mankind by insemination of a woman he had fashioned from the *mons veneris* of Earth. All this is repeated in Hawaiian legend, but as a story of humanized ancestors—thus told not in explication of the universe but as the origin of society. The proper names of the Hawaiian ancestors retain the cosmic intimations of their Maori counterparts: Wakea (Expansive Space, Zenith or Heavens) and Papa (Foundation Surface). And just as the god sprung from Heaven and Earth in the Maori tale inseminates a woman made from Earth, so the Hawaiian Wakea takes the daughter (Hoohokukalani) born to him of Papa, and from this original incest produces first, taro, and secondly, the ancestor of ruling chiefs. The structures are virtually homologous. But the Hawaiian legend is distinctively "brought to earth." In certain versions, it is set in Oahu. And rather than an account of the differentiation of elementary constituents of the universe, it tells of the differentiations that make the human order. For in the accompanying incidents and the sequel, other categories of society are established, such as the commoners, as well as the tabus separating men and women, the seasonal divisions and the periodic temple ceremonies *(kapu pule)*. Polynesian cosmogony becomes Hawaiian sociology (Malo 1951; Kamakau ms.; Beckwith 1970:293–307).

The same progression appears within Hawaiian folklore itself, when the legends are placed in the traditional sequence set by the great chiefly genealogies. A more mythic formulation of earlier epochs gives way to epic tales, even as continuity is maintained from the supernatural heroes of the remote past to recent chiefs through a series of logical permutations. Beckwith has neatly summarized this sequence (1919:303). The legendary protagonists of the most distant genealogical epochs are famous great gods. But in this period heaven and earth are not far apart. The conjunction of cosmic domains found, for example, in Maori cosmogony—union of Rangi and Papa—is functionally expressed in Hawaiian lore as the appearance of the gods in human affairs. The implication is that the celestial or subterranean realms are not distant, and the gods move easily between them and the earthly plane of man. Gradually, however, category by category, the supernatural heroes depart the mythical scene. First major gods such as Kane and Kanaloa withdraw to their own sphere, then successively, the demi-gods, the supernatural lizards *(mo'o)* and beast gods (e.g., Kamapuaa), and finally the miraculous little peoples *(menehune, mū, etc.)* likewise pass. There remain as legendary protagonists the great chiefs of yore, ancestors of the Islands' ruling lines.

The *mana* of the chiefly heroes is extraordinary, but more appropriate to a human nature than were the supernatural gifts of their predecessors. The chiefs win success by their subtlety, courage, skill and strength. Correspondingly, the plane of dramatic action in the legends rotates from the vertical to the horizontal. Rather than traveling between the earth and the realms above and below, the heroes demonstrate their prowess in adventurous voyages from distant lands, or between Hawaii and distant lands, often arriving from these fabled and invisible places with new goods, new cults and new heirs. Thus the well-known "voyaging" or "migration" period of Hawaiian folklore, set about 20 generations back from historic times (Fornander 1969). With the migrations, the notion of an origin place, an original homeland, is transferred also to distant places: the "lost land of Kane," the floating island Kuaihelani, and the like. Hence the very important concept of Kahiki "invisible lands beyond the horizon" carries the sense of an original time. (Handy notes the equivalent Marquesan usage, tai ou, meaning at once 'distant seas' and 'distant times': "It was impossible to tell whether there was in their minds a sense of great distance or great antiquity when they used these phrases" [1923:252].) But just as the Kauai chief who discussed these matters with Lt. Rickman of the Cook expedition was convinced that, as beings from Kahiki, the British had journeyed to the sun between their first and second visits to Hawaii, the overseas lands also retain the connotation of 'the above' (Rickman 1781:332). For at the horizon, the dome of the sky meets the border of the earth, and to voyage beyond is to break into the heavens. So also chiefs down to historic times maintained their celestial associations: lani 'heavens' is a common epithet for 'chief' (cf. Makemson 1938; Fornander 1916–1919 v.4:374).

At the final stages of legend, however, long distance voyaging ceases. The dramatic space contracts to the Hawaiian group. Chiefly movements are accordingly reduced to travels between the Hawaiian islands, and chiefly adventures to contests between local rivals. Still the genealogical tradition provides an invariant frame for all these permutations, articulating the latest of the human heroes with the greatest of the gods—and allowing the possibility that the latter will reappear in the persons of the former. "Gods and men are, in fact, to the Polynesian mind one family under different forms, the gods having superior control over certain phenomena, a control which they may impart to their offspring on earth" (Beckwith 1919:304).

Indeed the logic of divine classification works on the same principle of genus and species as the concept of descent, providing motivation for the principle of historical representation or incarnation even in the absence of demonstrable genealogical connection. Or rather, the functional similarity between gods and men can then become the basis of a genealogical supposition, as in the instance of Captain Cook. The great multitude of Hawaiian male gods, almost without exception, are classified as individual forms of four major classes whose "heads" are the generic gods, Ku, Lono, Kane and Kanaloa. God names therefore are typically binomials, with a stem composed of one of the four great names and a particularizing attribute (Valeri: n.d.). The Lono image of the Makahiki festival is, by most accounts, Lono-makua (Father-Lono) or Lono-i-ka-makahiki (Lono-of-the-Makahiki), names also associated with Cook. By the same principles, the appropriation of the reproductive powers of Earth by Sky, or of the daughter of Papa by Wakea, becomes the generic version of the theory of usurpation that was working in Hawaiian politico-ritual practice down to, and *including,* the advent of Captain James Cook:

> Stories and genealogies connect the Wakea-Papa line with the myth already noticed of a marriage between a high chief from a distant land and a native-born chiefess. A struggle is implied between an older line and a new order which imposes the separation of chiefs from commoners and both from a degraded slave class, and establishes the religious tabus. . . . Back of [the Wakea-Papa story] is the Polynesian mythical conception of a dark, formless spirit world presided over by the female element, and a world of form born out of the spirit world and to which it again returns, made visible and active in this human life through light [i.e., Wakea] as the impregnating male element. (Beckwith 1972:294, 306)

As these remarks suggest, the theory is *total* in the Maussian sense. At the great annual Makahiki festival, the concept of political usurpation is set in the context of a cosmological drama. The lost god-chief Lono returns to renew the fertility of the land, reclaiming it as his own, to be superseded again by the ruling chief and the sacrificial cult of Ku. Now Captain Cook's second visit to the Islands coincided with the annual return of Lono, and the treatment Hawaiians accorded him corresponded to the prescribed sequence of ritual events in the Makahiki Festival. The correspondence developed to its dramatic *dénouement:* the death of the god. Cook's fate was the historical image of a mythical theory, mediated by the correlation between his own practical rituals for dealing with "the natives" and Hawaiian ritual practices for dealing with "the gods."

CAPTAIN COOK AS LONO: MYTHICAL REALITIES AND HISTORICAL METAPHORS

Cook's first visit to Kauai and Niihau early in 1778 was certainly treated by Hawaiians as a divine appearance, but there is no indication in contemporaneous sources that he was immediately identified as Lono. Still, for Hawaiians, centuries of sacrifice had been rewarded: the very first man from Kauai to board HMS *Resolution* proceeded—without hesitation or the least trouble to conceal it—to pick up the ship's sounding line and carry it away. Halted by British incantations of private property, he was asked where he thought he was going. "I am only going to put it in my boat," he said (Cook *in* Beaglehole 1967:265). The cargo cult Melanesians later dreamed about these Polynesians for one fleeting instant realized: "they thought they had a right to anything they could lay their hands on," wrote Cook (Cook and King 1784 v.2:205). The Kauai people were soon disabused of the opinion. But according to Hawaiian tradition, the good news—along with such evidence of British *mana* as venereal disease and iron adzes—rapidly spread from island to island: "they have doors in the sides of their bodies [pockets] . . . into these openings they thrust their hands, and take thence many valuable things—their bodies are full of treasure" (Dibble 1909 [1843]:23).

The interpretation of this visitation as an advent of Lono, however, does not appear in the historical record until Cook's sojourn at Hawaii Island a year later, upon his return from the Northwest Coast. The *Resolution* and *Discovery* arrived off Maui on 26 November 1778; but Cook did not anchor or step ashore until 17 January 1779 at Kealakekua Bay, after circumnavigating the Island of Hawaii. There, as he was met at the beach and escorted by priests of Lono to the principal temple (Hikiau), the people retreating and prostrating before, he could hear in the priests' short declamation, "Erono!" [O Lono!]—an appellation given Cook at Hawaii Island specifically, according to Mr. King, and by which he was known to the day of his death.[4]

The Makahiki festival is marked by the appearance of the Pleiades on the horizon at sunset; in 1778, this would be about 18 November, a week before Cook appeared on the horizon (Makemson 1941; I'i 1959:72). The ritual sequence, however, is ordered on the Hawaiian lunar calendar, with periodic ceremonies from the last month of the cool season (Ikuwa in the Hawaii Island calendar) through the initial months of the warm season (Welehu, Makali'i [Pleiades] and Kaelo). I describe the ritual cycle in a condensed way, for comparison to Cook's adventures in Hawaii. The extant Hawaiian descriptions of the Makahiki date from the early to mid-nineteenth century, after the abolition of the traditional religion, and are based on recollections of the authors or their elders (Malo 1951; Kamakau *in* Fornander 1916–1919 v.6:34ff; I'i 1959; Kepelino 1932, 1977).

During the first stages of the Makahiki, the normal temple rituals—four tabu periods each lunar month—are progressively suspended for different classes of the population. The Ku cult, associated with the ruling chief and distinctively with human sacrifice, is thus put in abeyance, making way for the temporary ascendancy of Lono during the annual renewal of nature. An image of Lono—a cross-piece ensign, with white tapa cloth hanging from the horizontal bar (cf. Malo 1951:143–144; I'i 1959:70–72)—is carried, along with other gods, in ceremonial procession around each major island. The tour marks Lono's appropriation of the land. A general "tabu of Lono" is imposed, including a prohibition on war. The king and high priest are secluded, not to be seen for a certain period; the priest is also blindfolded, so as not to see the people's revelries. In the course of his circuit, Lono is ritually fed by the king and ruling chiefs at their domestic shrines, and receives their homages and offerings (rites of *hānaipū*). The ranking wives of the high chiefs bring gifts at this time, to beg in return Lono's gift of fertility, that they might bear a sacred child. Great offerings *(ho'okupu)* too are made by the people of each land district *(ahupua'a);* these are collected by the land supervisors *(konohiki),* testifying to Lono's proprietary right. In the wake of Lono's passage through each district, the people engage in sham battles—some of which apparently oppose them to chiefs—as well as feasting and other celebrations. Such scenes of the Makahiki are reminiscient of carnival and the Saturnalia, including also the sexual licenses taken by "the laughing people" (cf. I'i 1959:70–76).

The procession of Lono lasts 23 days (23 Welehu to 16 Makali'i) and is prescriptively a "right [hand] circuit," i.e., clockwise, with the right hand of the god inland toward the center of the island. According to Kamakau, a right circuit signifies possession or retention of the kingdom (1961:134; 1976:5). During this period, however, another god of similar design—the *akua poko* 'short god', as opposed to the Lono image, the *akua loa* or 'long god'—makes a tour to the ruling chief's own lands. But this is a "left circuit," signifying the loss of the kingdom. I take it that the contrast in gods and circuits represents the respective fate of Lono and the reigning king at this period of the annual cycle. On the day the Lono image returns to the temple of origin, the king comes to shore by canoe before the same temple. Disembarking, he is met by armed attendants of the god, one of whom successfully, though harmlessly, attains the ruler with a spear (rite of *kāli'i).* There follows a sham battle, apparently between the respective followers of king and god. Unfortunately, the sources are silent on the outcome of the battle, specification of which might remove the ambiguities of this apparent "ritual of rebellion." The spear that touches the king is said to lift the tabus on him. *Kāli'i,* the name of the rite, means 'to play (or act) the king'. This may be the moment of the king's reconquest (cf. Valeri: n.d.). On the other hand, the king is symbolically hit, and following the sham fight he enters the temple to offer a pig to the god and welcome him to "the land of us-two."

Within a few days, however, Lono himself suffers a ritual death. The

Makahiki image is dismantled, bound up and secluded in the temple, not to be seen again until the next year. An abundance of food, considered Lono's possession, is then gathered in a net of loose mesh (net of Maoloha) and ritually shaken to earth, i.e., falls from Lono's abode. A so-called "canoe of Lono" laden with offerings is subsequently set adrift to Kahiki. Thereupon the temples are progressively opened again for the Ku rituals, the ceremonies prominently featuring a ceremonial double or personal god of the king, Kahoalii (The-Companion-of-the-King, a god in human form).[5]

Kahoalii is specifically associated with rites of human sacrifice: among his other names were Kaukalia (Fearful) and Kokokakamake (Death-is-Near) (cf. Kamakau 1964:14, 20; Emerson 1915:203: Kepelino 1932:12; among others). Kahoalii figures again in the final rites of the Makahiki, during or shortly after the full moon of the month Kaelo. These ceremonies put a definitive end to certain tabus (as the interdiction on pork-eating by chiefs) that obtained while offerings to Ku had been suspended. A human sacrifice is offered and one of the eyes, along with the eye of a bonito, is swallowed by Kahoalii. In 1779, the closing ceremonies of the Makahiki would fall about the first of February ($\pm$ 1 day), and Cook left Kealakekua, a traditional place for these rites, early in the morning of 4 February. He thought he was leaving for good.

As this last notice suggests, it proves possible to collate the transactions of the Cook voyage, according to European calendar dates, with the ritual activities of the Makahiki as set forth in extant ethnographic descriptions by Hawaiian lunar dates. Computer calculation gives us the phases of the moon for the relevant period of 1778–1779, but the problem remains of equating Hawaiian lunar month names with the European dates at issue. The problem arises because a lunar calendar loses 11 days each solar year. It appears that the Hawaiians intercalated an extra 30-day month every three years to bring the lunar and solar calendars into rough correspondence, but another longer-term intercalation would also be necessary, about which we are presently uncertain. Nonetheless, for the time of Cook's visit, the correlation between the European calendar and Hawaii Island lunar months can be made with considerable assurance, thanks to the evidences of Hawaiian ritual practices noted by date in the chronicles of the voyage. To be precise (within a day or two), Cook's appearance off Maui on 26 November 1778 corresponded to 7 Welehu in the Hawaii calendar.

The correlation between the ritual movements of the Makahiki image Lono and the historical movements of Captain Cook in 1778–79 was not perfect, but it was sufficiently remarkable.[6] Cook began his circumnavigation of Hawaii Island on 2 December 1778, by Hawaiian reckoning 12 Welehu, the date of the final closing of the temples to Ku rituals.

(Indeed, the people on the shores of Kohala were waving white flags at the British ships, a sign that a ritual tabu was on.) Cook's progression around the Island, from Kohala to Kealakekua, was a "right circuit," thus parallel to the progression of Lono along the shore. Kealakekua, where Cook finally anchored, was the home of a large body of Lono priests; its main temple, Hikiau, was the place at which Lono traditionally began and ended his own circuit. Arriving there on 17 January 1779, Cook's circumnavigation took a longer period than Lono's own circuit—the later calculable as 13 December 1778 to 4 January 1779—but would have encompassed the god's progress. Upon landing, Cook was immediately escorted to the great temple of Hikiau, where he allowed himself to be led by priests through an elaborate set of rites, characterized in both British and Hawaiian accounts as "adoration" or "worship."

One segment of these rites corresponded, detail by detail, to the *hānaipū:* the customary homage offered to the image of Lono by ranking chiefs during the gods procession (cf. Cook and King 1784 v.3:8–9 and Beaglehole 1967:506 with I'i 1959:75 and Fornander 1916–1919 v.6:40–43). Cook first of all was made to imitate by his own posture the shape of the Makahiki image while a pig was offered to him, Mr. King and a priest holding his outstretched arms (i.e., the crosspiece of the Lono image). The offering prayer was made by a group of Lono priests chanting responses to their leader, one "Kaireekea." "We observed," King wrote, "that after every response, their parts became gradually shorter, till, toward the close, Kaireekea's consisted of only two or three words, which the rest answered by the word *Orono* [O Lono]" (Cook and King 1784, v.3:8). This choral counterpoint, punctuated by salutation of the god, is likewise attested for the reception of Lono at the eating house or the domestic shrine *(mua)* of the chief. A feast and kava were then prepared for Cook, as for the Makahiki image. Following the ritual precedure appropriate to the latter, the priest Kaireekea anointed Cook with coconut oil, a rite distinctive of Lono (as opposed to the anointing of Ku with the grease of sacrificial victims). Another priest, "Koah," this one associated with the ruling chief Kalaniopuu, thereupon proceeded to feed Cook by hand, just as the chief feeds the Makahiki image (i.e., the bearer) at the *hānaipū* ceremony. Cook could not bring himself to swallow the food so respectfully tendered and shortly after left the temple. But the whole *hānaipū* rite was repeated two days later when he visited the Lono temple at Kealakekua (Hale o Lono); and still again on that day at another shrine five miles south—apparently the Hale-o-Keawe (House-of-Keawe), sacred repository of the ancestral bones of the island's ruling line (Samwell *in* Beaglehole 1967:1161–1162).

Kalaniopuu, the King (or ruling chief) of Hawaii, was on Maui while all this was happening in and about Kealakekua. The King finally arrived at Kealakekua on 25 January 1779, a date that would be subsequent to certain "purification" rituals by which the ruler makes transition back to normal (Ku) status. Now if the Makahiki was on schedule, as it appears, the definitive closing rituals, involving human sacrifice, would take place on 30 January to 1 February (± one day). Sometime after, the wooden fence, houses and images of the temple would be completely refurbished for Ku rites. On 1 February, William Watman, seaman, died aboard the *Resolution*. At the request of the Hawaiian chiefs—or by some report, of the King—Watman was buried that afternoon in the great temple of Hikiau. Messrs. Cook and King read the divine service with Hawaiian priests in rapt attendance. The British rituals ended, the Hawaiian priests proceeded to throw pigs and other offerings into the grave—a pious office they continued to render, according to Mr. King, for three nights. Also on 1 February, the British, with permission of the priests, carried off the wooden fence and images of the temple (save the main image of Ku) for firewood. On 2 February, King writes that the chiefs were now beginning to ask when the British would be leaving—and were relieved to learn their departure was imminent. Cook, however, did promise to come back next year (Cook and King 1784 v.3:30)! Everything was indeed proceeding historically right on ritual schedule.

THE DEATH AND APPROPRIATION OF THE GOD

To appreciate the historical-ritual sequel, it has to be considered that the Captain and the King, Cook and Kalaniopuu, representing respectively Lono and Ku, were natural rivals for Hawaiian power.[7] If Cook were Lono, he had come back to claim his own. Thus returning, he evoked in an ominous mode (a revenge or restoration) the whole theory of god-chiefs come from Kahiki to depose the indigenous ruling line. But as this same theory was represented in the Makahiki, it would all work out to the benefit of the Hawaiian ruler—so long as Cook adhered to the ritual calendar and played the part of the god that lost.[8] In late January 1779, the ascending political curve of Ku (Kalaniopuu) as represented in the Makahiki ceremonies intersected with the declining course of Lono (Cook), on his way out again to Kahiki. Cook obliged by leaving almost at the precise end of the Makahiki period, just when the chiefs became anxious to know when he was going. A few days later, however, the ritual calendar intersected with another field of causation: the *Resolution* unfortunately sprung her foremast, and the ships put back again to Kealakekua, arriving on the 11th of February.

Cook was now *hors catégorie*. Lono had come and bestowed his riches in iron, already largely in the hands of ranking chiefs—who had thus successfully weathered his passage and regained the land. Then he departed, presumably to return again a year later with the Pleiades. The abrupt reappearance of the ships was a contradiction to all that had gone before. Relations between the Europeans and Hawaiians degenerated immediately and rapidly. The Hawaiians committed a series of thefts, of augmenting boldness and magnitude—"insolence," as the British deemed it. Such thefts the British already knew to be linked to chiefs, either directly or indirectly, but the inclination had not been marked since the first hectic days at Kealakekua when 10,000 Hawaiians crowded on the waters and shores of the Bay—and all over the ships—in exuberant welcome of Lono. The welcome of 17 January 1779 had been the greatest reception any European voyager ever had in this Ocean: "Anchored in 17^{fms} black sand having towed and sailed in, amidst an Innumerable Number of Canoes, the people in which were singing and rejoicing all the way" (Riou Log: 17 January 1779). Now, on 11 February, the Bay was quiet, relatively empty of people and these, according to some accounts, showed nothing like the same amicability. And whereas before, the problem of theft had been resolved within a few days, largely through the enlistment of local chiefs in the regulation of exchange, now thefts became more serious daily. And at least one of the same chiefs (Palea, a "favorite" of the King) was a main culprit, so far as the British could ascertain. More, the thefts gave rise to unprecedented violence, including an incident on 13 February in which an unarmed British party was soundly drubbed. That night the cutter of the *Discovery* was stolen.

Cook resolved upon measures that could only exacerbate the political-ritual oppositions. One might say that he invoked his own native political rituals: the famous colonial disposition to "find the chief." Blockading the Bay so that no canoes might leave, he landed with a party of marines to take King Kalaniopuu hostage against the return of the cutter. As Cook was leading the apparently willing Kalaniopuu to a ship's boat near the shore, the King's wife and several notables intervened. What they said to the old King gave him pause. He refused to go on, sat down on the ground and appeared now "dejected and frightened." Cook decided to abandon the hostage plan, but just then news reached the crowd gathered at the scene that a chief had been killed trying to leave the Bay. At approximately the same time, Cook was forced to fire (ineffectively) at a man threatening him with a long iron dagger. (This would also be a chief, as the iron daggers the British put into trade, highly coveted and constantly affected as signs of rank, quickly came into the chiefs' possession.) The several accounts of what followed are confused, but all agree that the crowd took up arms, passed on to the attack and Cook fell—to the blow, again, of an iron dagger. It was a ritual murder, in the end collectively administered: upwards of a hundred Hawaiians rushed upon the fallen god to have a part in his death.

The killing of Captain Cook was not premeditated by the Hawaiians. But neither was it an accident, structurally speaking. It was the Makahiki in an historical form. Nor was the historic aftermath a simple empirical *sequitur* to the event. Within 48 hours of Cook's death, two priests of Lono stole out to HMS *Resolution*—at risk of vengeance both from the British and their own ruling chiefs—bearing a piece of his body. Handing it over to the British with expressions of great sorrow, they asked when Lono "would come again?" (Cook and King 1784 v.3:69). It was a question British voyagers would hear from other Hawaiians, not only at this time but again in later years (Colnett Journals:1 April 1791; cf. Sahlins 1979). Cook's bones were actually returned to the British on 21 and 22 February 1779, and committed by them to the waters of Kealekekua Bay—or so it seemed. For in the early nineteenth century the bones reappear, wrapped in the sennit casket of apotheosized chiefs, being carried around the Island of Hawaii by priests of Lono in the annual rites of the Makahiki. He had "come again" (Martin 1817 v.2:66–67; Ellis 1828:120; Mathison 1825:431–32).

"When one god vanquishes another," Hubert and Mauss observed, "he perpetuates the memory of his victory by the inauguration of a cult" (1964:89). Usurpation, we have seen, is the very principle of political legitimacy in the Hawaiian system. "Every chief acts as a conqueror when he comes to power," Hawaiians say. And even if he has not actually killed his predecessor, he is presumed to have poisoned him: just as for some years visiting Europeans were told that Kamehameha had poisoned Kalaniopuu, in revenge of an insult to himself—or, as he claimed, in revenge of the death of Captain Cook (Meares 1790:344). Kamehameha's story was at once false and yet characteristic twice-over of the Hawaiian theory of chieftainship (even apart from the dividends in good will he might have been seeking by retailing it to passing Europeans). The theory is, as Hocart (1927) says more generally of such magical kings, that the succession is the celebration of a victory. The dead chief is by implication a transgressor of the tabus and an oppressor of the people. Slaying him, his successor not only recreates the established order, he thereupon appropriates the death as a claim of "quasi-normal" succession. Thus the sense of Kamehameha's story about the poisoning of Kalaniopuu, and also of the way that Kalaniopuu in practice treated the remains of Captain Cook.

Hawaiian treatments of the chiefly dead seem to follow no simple rule. Among the variant practices, however, are two analogous forms, applicable respectively to ruling chiefs who die a "natural death" and rival chiefs taken in battle and offered in sacrifice. From the perspective of the successor, the status of these two is indeed analogous, their death in either case is his victory, and the disposition of the corpse in different ways is designed to harness the powers of the dead to the *mana* of the quick. Before the sacrifice, a defeated rival is singed on an open hearth, like a pig. Normally the body is allowed to rot on the altar, but it may be taken outside the temple and baked to facilitate removal of the flesh. In either event, the bones of great rivals are disarticulated and distributed as trophies among paramount's followers, to be fixed in their ritual regalia, the extent and character of this distribution apparently varying with the intent and necessity to share power. The skull of the victim is normally reserved to the god, the long bones and mandible to the ruling chief. Such was the fate of Captain Cook, according to contemporary accounts. Consecrated in sacrifice by his rival Kalaniopuu, his remains were cooked and the bones distributed to lesser chiefs, the king retaining the long bones (Samwell 1967:1215; Cook and King 1784 v.3:66; Valeri n.d.).

The treatment of the long bones in particular makes a connection with the mortuary rites of chiefs died in office. These rites enshrine the dead ruler as the ancestral spirit *('aumākua)* of his successor. The body is allowed to decompose or it is cooked for 10 days in a shallow oven to disengage the flesh. The long bones and skull are subsequently placed in a sennit casket covered with red feathers, accompanied by temple rites that transform the dead king into a true god of the land *(akua maoli)*. The casket is then deposited in a temple shrine, where it resides as the guardian of royal successors. Such is the form, complete with feathered casket, in which Cook appears in historical accounts of the early nineteenth century (e.g., Ellis 1828:120). Cook was thus historically sacrificed as a rival, to be ideologically recuperated at a later time as an ancestor. But then, the behavior of Kalaniopuu immediately after Cook's death already suggests an amalgam of the two forms. Kalaniopuu went directly into seclusion, accompanied by Kamehameha and the high priest of Lono: the appropriate ritual procedure for the heir of a deceased king, as it is also the annual practice of the living king following the dismantling of the Lono image during the Makahiki (Cook and King 1784 v.3:66, 68, 78; Beaglehole 1967:1215; Law Journal:18 February 1779; cf. Malo 1951:104–106).

In 1793, Lt. Peter Puget of Vancouver's squadron had an important interview with the high priest of the temple at Kealakekua where Cook had been ritually received as Lono fourteen years earlier. The priest told Puget the story of Paao, ascribing to it the origin of the existing religion—''their Religion underwent a total change by the Arrival of a Man from Taitah [Kahiki], who was suffered to land. His visit produced the morai ['temple'] & the present established form of worship, no other

account could the Priest give of its origin.'' Thereupon as if in logical ap-
position, the priest went on to discuss the status of Captain Cook:
''Their gods he told us were numerous and Good. One he distinguished
as superior to the Rest, that always accompanied the King
[Kamehameha]. It has the same name as that given to Captain Cook.''
Earlier in the interview, the priest had analyzed Cook's death, attributing
it to a cause that also seems logically motivated by the same theory—if
historically unsupportable. Cook died, the priest said, because he had
taken off the wooden palings and images of the temple for firewood. In
fact no resentment had been shown, either by priests or people, at the
time the wood was removed—according to Mr. King, who personally arranged and supervised the transaction (Beaglehole 1967:516; Cook and
King 1784 v.3:25-26). But if the interpretation was historically inaccurate as of 1 February 1779, it had become true as of 1793. Cook-Lono
was a tabu transgressor. The reanalysis was not simply in justification of
what the Hawaiians had done to him. It signified his present position as a
divine guardian—the most important, said the priest—of the Hawaiian
ruling chief. Mediated by the sacrifice of Cook, the *mana* of the
Hawaiian paramount had become British—hence the role of the British
in Hawaiian politics in the decades that followed, despite their superces-
sion in Hawaiian economics.

By 1800-1810, Americans dominated Hawaii's external commerce
(Bradley 1968; Howay 1930-1934; Morgan 1948). Yet the
means—indeed the disposition—by which the great Kamehameha turned
that commerce into practical account was his own special relation to
British power. Inheritor of Cook's murder and thus of his *mana,*
Kamehameha embarked on an explicit and distinctive policy of friendship, royal generosity and honest exchange with British and other foreign
visitors. He also took care to promote the production necessary for
trade. After 1791, the troubles European vessels experienced with the
chiefs of other Hawaiian Islands were practically unknown in
Kamehameha's domains. But then, these chiefs (or their predecessors)
had not had the good fortune to kill the Great Navigator. Transmitted
through the manes of Captain Cook, Kamehameha's special relation to
European *mana* gave him enough of it, in the form of guns, ships, and
resident advisors, to conquer the Islands.

Kamehameha's European policy was strongly in evidence from the
time foreign contacts resumed in the latter 1780s, when several British
fur traders visited Hawaii (cf. Meares 1790). It was even more pro-
nounced in the course of Vancouver's sojourns of 1793 and 1794. He
''declares it his most solemn determination,'' according to Mr. Bell of
the Vancouver expedition, ''never to molest or disturb the weakest vessel
that comes to Karakakoo [Kealakekua], or where he himself is, on the

contrary to do everything he can to make their stay among them comfortable—he laments in the most pathetic terms the death of Captain Cook, and seems to hold his memory in the utmost veneration" (1929–1930 I(6):84). True that Kamehameha had at the time good advice to this effect from the resident Englishmen John Young and Isaac Davis. But such was already a symptom of the European policy, since he had saved these two from the subordinate chiefs who had taken the trading vessel *Fair American* in 1790, and upbraided the chiefs for their attack on the shipping.[9]

This generous reception of foreign merchant and naval vessels on Kamehameha's part was the theory of the Makahiki transposed by the death of Cook into a register of practice. The Makahiki already dramatizes the periodic appropriation by the conquering chief of the ultrahuman powers of growth and reproduction, bound up, as by the food net of Maoloha, in distant and heavenly space (Kahiki). Interesting then, that early nineteenth century myths of the Makahiki, latterly elaborated to assimilate Captain Cook within the traditional code, take on elements of a millenial cargo cult. Byron speaks of the Hawaiian identification of Cook with Lono, as he heard of it in 1825;

> As they confidently expected that the return of Lono was to confer some immediate and important benefit, they eagerly embraced the idea [when Cook arrived], that the blessed era was come; and that all the knowledge which they believed, on the faith of tradition, they had lost should be restored, and new arts and comforts taught them by the inhabitants of the floating islands [Cook's ships]. (Byron 1826:27)

The cargo cult of the initial moment of Hawaiian-British contact—"their bodies are full of treasure"—endures, although by virtue of Cook's death in a differentiated mode, of unique benefit to the King and Island of Hawaii. It informs the actual organization of *praxis,* out of which develops the historical organization of the polity. For in the particular instance of Kamehameha, the continuity between cosmology and commerce might not only be logically or metaphorically founded, but metonymically motivated by the murder of Captain Cook. Among the rival chiefs of the Islands, Kamehameha had the most to fear from the event—and the historical accounts document his trepidations—but also then the most to gain, by virtue of an exclusive claim to objectify it. Objectified at first in myth, ritual and exchange, Kamehameha's "English connection" survived long after the conquest it facilitated, to become an essential concept of his sovereignty.

The conquest was largely completed by 1795, when Kamehameha took Maui, Molokai and Oahu. The year before, however, on Vancouver's urging he had gone so far as to cede the Island of Hawaii to his "loving brother" King George—for so Kamehameha considered him (Bell 1929–1930 II(2):119; Franchère 1969:63; Ross 1849:35). The Cession of 1794 was rejected by Vancouver's Government. Nonetheless, Kamehameha and his successor Liholiho continued to think of themselves as subjects of His British Majesty—or at least under the latter's protection—well into the nineteenth century. The British colors were flying from Kamehameha's house and canoe even before the Cession of 1794, and so they were still in 1807 (Iselin n.d.: 75), 1809 (Campbell 1819:129) and even later (Tyreman and Bennet 1831:436). In 1822, Liholiho still "professes openly to hold his dominions under the King of England" (Tyreman and Bennet 1831:472); "his islands belonged to the King of Great Britain," he told Mathison (1825:366). Two years later Liholiho died of measles in London, where he had gone to secure the help of his father's brother, King George (now IV) against the economic and political encroachments of his own chiefs—who, moreover, had entered into working relationship with the American missionaries (cf. Bradley 1968; Kuykendall 1968). When some of the first formal laws were enacted by the fledgling state in 1827, the chiefs, under pressure from those loyal to the throne, decided at one point they would have to be ratified by the British Sovereign before they could take effect (Kuykendall 1968:125; cf. Bryon 1826:133). Indeed, to this day the Union Jack flies in the upper left-hand corner of the state flag of Hawaii.

CHIEFS AND EUROPEANS, OR THE
FURTHER HISTORY OF COOKING

One might say that Kamehameha had effected a revolution in Hawaiian theology and politics. But it was not the first of its kind. The priest did tell Puget the story of Paao. Nor was this the last time Paao, or the theory of a religiously-inspired political usurpation, came into play in Hawaiian history. The difficulties experienced by the American missionaries during the years immediately following their arrival in 1820 might be attributed, at least in part, to their mythological predecessor. It proved to be true enough that the American *kahuna* 'priests' were the harbingers of a new order, destined to bring down both king and kingdom. Giving credence to the counsel he received from his English friends in particular, King Liholiho at first only reluctantly and provisionally agreed to allow American missionaries on his soil. The missionaries soon became aware of the King's fears that they were the vanguard of an American plot to seize the Islands. Parallels were being drawn to the fate of the native people of America and to the reported domination of Tahitians by Christian missionaries (A.B.C.F.M. Missionaries 1821:114ff; Tyreman and Bennet 1831:472; Hunnewell to Ellis 20 January 1831; Hunnewell 1864; Bradley 1968:126). Rumor after rumor fills the trader and missionary journals of the 1820s concerning American conspiracies against Hawaiian power, such as the following:

> Natives put a story in circulation that the mission houses were burnt in Mowee [Maui] the Mission sent off. Pitt [Kalaimoku, the "Prime Minister"] gone to Owhyhee [Hawaii] to send them forever from that Island, because the mission gave the young prince [Kauikeaouli, later Kamehameha III] and princess [Nahienaena] shit to eat. It appeared they were at the mission house and were offered bread and butter—the natives who were standing about the Prince not being acquainted with butter raised the report as above. (Reynolds Journal:25 April 1824)

The mention of "Billy Pitt" is an indication—only apparently paradoxical—of the same Hawaiian theory of political and cosmic order, and of its capacity to encompass historical circumstances within received relationships. Billy Pitt was an Hawaiian (a.k.a. Kalaimoku) who ran the Islands under Kamehameha and Liholiho in the early nineteenth century, with the help of his classificatory brothers "Cox" (Kahekili Keeaumoku) and "John Adams" (Kuakini). These were not isolated instances of the chiefs taking consciousness of themselves as prominent Europeans. Many Hawaiians, noble and not quite so noble, chose such appelations of their own will, and like Billy Pitt insisted on being known by them. Already by 1793, three of the principal ruling chiefs had named their sons and heirs "King George" (Bell 1929–1930, I(5):64). The American trader Ross Cox describes the Honolulu scene at a gala foot race staged in 1812:

> At the race course I observed Billy Pitt, George Washington and Billy Cobbet walking together in the most familiar manner, and apparently engaged in confidential conversation; while in the center of another group, Charley Fox, Thomas Jefferson, James Madison, Bonnepart, and Tom Paine were seen to be on equally friendly terms with each other. (Cox 1832:44)

This apparently headlong rush to their own cultural doom on the chiefs' part, this kind of "acculturation," can be shown to reflect basic Hawaiian principles, and, by virtue of these principles, to be selective rather than indiscriminate. For in realizing themselves as European chiefs, the Hawaiian nobility reproduced a customary distinction between themselves and the underlying population. We have seen other evidence of the legendary differentiation of chiefs as divine invaders from an overseas spiritual realm (Kahiki). The chiefly ancestors, moreover, had displaced the original gods, and appropriated from them important cultural gifts: often by chicanery, as Maui (the trickster) had stolen fire from the gods—which helps account for the chiefly disposition toward theft noted in the Cook chronicles. So in the historical period, with a new godly power from Kahiki loose upon the land, the continuity of chiefly status depended on a deployment of the myth as practice. One would need to acquire things European, if necessary by force or guile. The chiefs showed an immediate interest in, and the capacity to adopt, signs of European civilization. The alternative, tradition told, was that they would be devoured.

The process by which chiefs appropriated European modes of living yields insight into a certain intercultural play of structure. The Hawaiian symbolic proportion—chiefs are to the people as the Europeans were to Hawaiians in general—entered into relationship with corresponding distinctions within European culture to render these historically salient. Specific European customs, objects and attitudes became prominent sites of historical interest and action. A basic intercultural agreement was reached about the value of the differences between Europeans and Hawaiians, because if for the foreigners these signified the opposition between "civilization" and "barbarism," so did the analogous Hawaiian distinction between chiefs and commoners represent a difference between culture and nature. The chiefs were differentiated from the common people *(maka'āinana)* by a higher degree of culture, just as the British thought themselves distinguished from the Hawaiians. Immigrants likewise from the spiritual realm, the Hawaiian chiefs had imposed the original tabus, which is to say the separations and distinctions that constitute a cultural order. Yet even more serendipitous, Hawaiians and foreigners could agree on the decisive practical indices of the passage from nature to culture, barbarism to civilization.

For both, it was important how and whether one was dressed, how and what one ate, how one was housed. The everyday signs of culture consisted of adherence to certain domestic proprieties. Hence the classical anthropological domains of the culture/nature distinction—clothing, housing, cooking—became critical areas of the so-called acculturation. Throughout Vancouver's visit of 1793, Kamehameha posted a personal servant to the galley of the *Discovery* as a kind of apprentice chef, to learn the British techniques of cooking. When the squadron was leaving, Kamehamea requested of Vancouver a bed, plates, knives, forks, and kitchen utensils. Going aboard the *Chatham,* he asked Puget for the same sorts of goods, refusing all other gifts. Mr. Manby observed:

> And now that he was in possession of the requisites of the table, a tolerable cook and every kind of implement for culinary purposes, the Monarch boasted with pride and satisfaction that he should now live like King George. (Manby 1929 I(3):46)

Great chiefs of the Islands never tired of asking early European visitors if King George lived as well as they, or vice versa. The European clothing they could affect was another indicative sign of their sophistication (cf. Sahlins 1977). Nineteenth century traders, missionaries and voyagers often remarked on how fashion-conscious the Hawaiians were. As it were, a significant contrast within the Hawaiian order, between chiefs and commoners, was transposed to and realized as a differentiation in its circumstances: an analogous contrast of "finery" in the culture of confrontation.

The Hawaiian chiefs seized upon the European distinctions between "plain" and "fancy" cloth to mark their own distance from the common people. The tendency was especially noticeable after Kemehameha's death in 1819, as a tactic in the ensuing conflict between ranking chiefs within the cadre of the early nineteenth century state. European *mana* in the form of domestic possessions now replaced military supplies as the principal means of aristocratic competition. Status was played out in the brightest silks of China and the finest textiles of New England. Nor would the chiefs at this period dip into accumulated political capital: to reduce their growing stores of clothing would be symptomatic of weakness; if need be they would rather go further into debt to acquire more of the same kinds of things as they already possessed in surfeit (Hammatt Journal:18 August 1823).[10] In the 1820s, the acquisition of fashionable clothing assumed orgiastic proportions. The proceeds of the sandalwood trade lie rotting in chiefly storehouses of cloth, to be dumped finally in the ocean.

Yet, again, one is in the presence of something familiarly Hawaiian: a structure of the long run—*mana*. Perhaps most essentially, *mana* is the creative power Hawaiians describe as making visible what is invisible, causing things to be seen, which is the same as making them known or giving them form. Hence the divine *mana* of chiefs is manifest in their brilliance, their shining. This, as much as corpulence, was the "beauty" that marked a chiefly status. The connection of great chiefs with the inseminating power of light and the sun is a corollary concept (cf. the story of Kila, Fornander 1916–1919 v.4:168). Hawaiian chiefs, we have seen, descend from Wakea, personification of the sun at high noon *(awakea)*. Thus the prostration tabu of the most sacred chiefs: like the sun, they could not be gazed upon without injury. Commoners accordingly were *makawela* 'burnt eyes'—just as the eyes of those who violated the chief's tabus were swallowed in sacrificial rites by Kahoali'i, the ceremonial double of the ruling chief (cf. Valeri n.d.). To the extent, then, of the Hawaiian market, the European mode of production and trade in the 1820s was organized by the Polynesian conception of *mana*.

The content of the system changes but not its norms. Yet only in certain respects and appearances is it true that the more it changes the more

it remains the same. A view of history that was content to see in the formation of classes and the state—no less has been entailed in this discussion—merely the reproduction of the traditional structure would arbitrarily limit the powers of an anthropological understanding. Cultural
theory has no need to be embarrassed in the face of structural change, as
some have claimed; nor is it condemned to a concern merely with the
"superstructural" foam on the wave of history.

3 Transformation
Structure and Practice

Hawaiian culture did not merely reproduce itself in the early years of European contact and the kingdom. In the course of reproducing that contact in its own image, the culture changed radically and decisively. The received system did enter into a dialectic with practice. The strong claim of a structuralist understanding does not consist in ignoring that dialectic. Rather, the interaction of system and event is itself susceptible of structural account, that is, as a meaningful process.

My aim is to demonstrate such historical uses of structural theory. I examine a certain interplay between pragmatic "structures of the conjuncture" and the received cultural order, as mediated by the constituted interests of the historical actors. The exposition begins with a paradigmatic example, an incident again from the initial days of contact between Captain Cook and the Hawaiians.

INCIDENT AT KAUAI: FUNCTIONAL REVALUATION

The first anchorage of the *Resolution* and *Discovery* in the Sandwich Islands was at Waimea Bay, Kauai, on 20 January 1778. On the 23rd, however, the *Resolution* under Cook lost her berth while trying to shift to a more sheltered location and was driven to sea, leaving the *Discovery*, Captain James Clerke, alone in the Bay. Next morning found the latter ship surrounded by a great many Hawaiian canoes, occupied by ordinary people engaged in a traffic of provisions for British iron, when abruptly the large double canoe of a chief appeared and ordered the others away.

But "without ceremony" or "regard" for the smaller vessels that could not move off quickly enough, the chief's canoe "ran against, or over them, without endeavoring in the least, to avoid them" (King Log:29 January 1778; Cook and King 1784 v.2:245–246). The occupants of four canoes were left swimming in the wreckage (Burney Journal:24 January 1778).

The chief was Kaneoneo (known originally to the British as "Kamahano"). Grandson of the ruling chief of Oahu, Kaneoneo was then, or had been shortly before, the consort of the ranking chiefess of Kauai. He was also at this moment competing for the supremacy of Kauai with another of the chiefess's husbands (Kaeo, half brother of the Maui paramount). But above all, Kaneoneo was a sacred chief of the highest tabus: offspring of a brother-sister union *(pi'o)*. Such a one is "called divine, *akua*" (Malo 1951:54); he is "fire, heat and raging blazes" (Kamakau 1964:4). When he goes abroad, the people must fall prostrate until he passes *(kapu moe),* the posture also of human victims on the altars of sacrifice. Kaneoneo was one of the few chiefs of the time—Captain Cook also among them—entitled to this, the highest Hawaiian form of obeisance. Which was why he ran over the people's canoes. If Kaneoneo's action seems unnecessarily high-handed, still the people had been slow to move off as ordered. For they were caught in an Hawaiian double-bind: prostrating face down in their canoes for the passage of the sacred chief, they could not also get out of his way.

Kaneoneo's relation to Captain Clerke was no less contradictory—for reasons that can be judged equally traditional. If Clerke were a godlike being from Kahiki, descending upon the Islands with iron and other marvelous goods, he was as much a potential rival and danger to the Hawaiian chief as a source of desirable *mana.* Every action of Kaneoneo's attendants aboard the *Discovery* testified to the ambiguities. Nor would Clerke's behavior disconfirm them, since he managed at once to violate the chief's tabus and present him some remarkable things.

Kaneoneo was attended by a retinue of lesser chiefs and men, but distinguished from these by a feather cloak thrown over his shoulders, while they wore loincloths only. Clerke wrote that never in all his life had he seen "a Person paid such abject Homage to; most of the Indians [i.e., Hawaiians] that were in the Vessel jumped overboard and hurried away in their Canoes when they saw him coming, the rest prostrated themselves before him, as soon as he got on board" (Clerke Log:24 January 1778). In fact he never exactly got on board. He was handed up the ship's side by his attendants who then immediately linked arms to form a protective circle around him on the gangway, and suffered no one but Clerke to approach him. Nothing could induce the chief's attendants to allow him to go below or even move from the spot, and after a short while he was carried down to his canoe by his people.

Clerke's reaction was friendly British gesture—which violated the strictest Hawaiian tabus on the person of a sacred chief. But then, Clerke was a down-to-earth man; unlike Cook, he could never tolerate the abject signs of homage the Hawaiians were always willing to give him. This time, "I was very desirous of laughing them out of their ridiculous fears; I said all I could, then took him by the hand and clapp'd him on the shoulder; upon which they [Kaneoneo's attendants] gently took away my hand and beg'd I would not touch him. There were at least half a score of principal people about him, who took as much care in getting him in and out of their canoe, as tho' a drop of salt water would have destroyed him." Kaneoneo presented a handsomely carved kava bowl and a large hog to Clerke, receiving in return a large cut-glass bowl, some red cloth and, "what he prized more than all," some very long nails (Clerke Log:24 January 1778).

The point I make of this anecdote is that the relationships generated in practical action, although motivated by the traditional self-conceptions of the actors, may in fact functionally revalue those conceptions. Nothing guarantees that the situations encountered in practice will stereotypically follow from the cultural categories by which the circumstances are interpreted and acted upon. Practice, rather, has its own dynamics—a "structure of the conjuncture"—which meaningfully defines the persons and the objects that are parties to it. And these contextual values, if unlike the definitions culturally presupposed, have the capacity then of working back on the conventional values. Entailing unprecedented relations between the acting subjects, mutually and by relation to objects, practice entails unprecedented objectifications of categories.

Everything that was done by the English and the Hawaiians was appropriately done, according to their own determinations of social persons, their interests and intentions. Yet the effect of thus putting culture into practice was to give some significance to the actors and actions that had not been traditionally envisioned. This functional effect is fairly self-evident in considering what (unintended) meaning a British gesture might have for an Hawaiian or vice versa. More radical are the effects on Hawaiian order itself, notably on the relations between chiefs and commoners. The arrival of the British occasioned an uncustomary violence between them. Hence even though, in proceeding upon their respective self-definitions, chiefs and commoners were reproducing the relationships that characterized them, they were also putting these relationships in jeopardy.

The difference in response of chiefs and people to the British presence is intelligible from the received structure. If the people unhesitatingly flocked to the ships and entered into commerce with them, such conduct is consistent with the Hawaiian notion of *'imi haku* 'seeking a lord'. We shall see that the same was an important motivation for the remarkable readiness—indeed the importunate demands—of ordinary Hawaiian women for sexual congress with European seamen. Behind this lay a system of landholding and personal security that depended, not on corporate lineage membership—for such was absent in Hawaii—but on the benevolent disposition of higher powers: chiefs and gods. On the other hand, the ambivalence of chiefs with regard to their divine visitors from Kahiki is also understandable from custom. Time and time again the chiefs approached European ships only several days after their arrival, and with a display at once of dignity, power and circumspection. The same kind of ambivalence, we already know, had its role in the death of Cook. But if the chiefs were hesitant, their own status *vis-à-vis* the people required a privileged access to the foreigners and their godly treasure. They would have to take priority in the mediation of foreign contact and exchange, whatever the risks of dealing with sharks that travel on land. Each party, chiefs and commoners, thus acted on interests pertinent to their social position, and in a way that would maintain the categorical differences between them.

Yet the effect was a degree and form of opposition that would not characterize relations between them in the normal course. In fact, if not in myth, the advent of ultrahuman beings from Kahiki was not an ordinary occurrence. Ordinarily, in fact, there would be no occasion for a tabu chief to run down his people's canoes, since the rule is that when a fleet goes out no canoe should take the lead on the chief's—not to mention that chiefs of the greatest tabus (such as the *kapu moe* held by Kaneoneo) should normally go outdoors only at night, just to avoid, it is said, such general inconvenience or danger to the people (cf. Malo 1951:54). There is evidence even in the present instance of an attempt to avoid the problem. The log of Thomas Edgar, master of the *Discovery,* reads that on the morning of 24 January at first no canoes came off to the ship, to the surprise of the British, and Hawaiians on board said their King was coming. Occurrences of this sort are frequently remarked in later voyages: the waters are cleared by the imposition of a tabu, to make way for the privileged advent of the chief. It may be that we have here the first example of what is also documented for later voyages—that the tabu is violated by daring commoners. In any event, the attempt to clear failed, and chiefs and people, each following their rightful course and dispositions, down to the niceties of prostration that immobilized the people, came into collision.

I take this incident as a paradigm, not only of the unfolding relations between chiefs and commoners, but of the historical stress put upon the entire Hawaiian scheme of social distinctions, together with its cosmological values. The categories were redefined by their differential relationships to the European presence. Men in opposition to women, priests to chiefs, *kaukau ali'i* lesser chiefs' to *ali'i nui* 'greater chiefs'—or, at other levels, the windward islands of Hawaii and Maui in contrast to Oahu, the exposed coasts vs. the sheltered ports, the valleys that support taro as opposed to those that grow yams, the pigs (which the Europeans would eat) by relation to the dogs (which they would not)—all these categorical distinctions proved vulnerable to a pragmatic revaluation. No matter that the motivation for the differential responses of men and women or commoners and chiefs to the foreigners was altogether Hawaiian. The content picked up in the experience meant that the relationships between them would never again be the same. Returning from ship to shore, especially from trade to domestic consumption—in short, from practice to structure—the effects become systemic. An alteration in the relationship between given categories affects their possible relationships to other categories. The structure, as a set of relationships among relationships, is transformed.

I examine in detail one such complex of transformations. It concerns the development of a certain solidarity between ordinary men and women as commoners, by opposition to the chiefly and priestly powers-that-be. At issue is an unprecedented class formation. Also at issue is the degeneration of the tabus which had defined these traditional distinctions. We can briefly follow the ritual dissolution to its famous *dénouement,* the abolition of the tabu system under chiefly aegis in 1819, before the first Christian missionary had set foot on the Islands. This end came of the same type of process among the chiefs as had set them in opposition to the commoners: differential relations to the Europeans that radically altered the correlation of categories within the ruling group.

THE COMMERCE OF CULTURAL CATEGORIES:
MEN, WOMEN AND CHIEFS

The Hawaiians had at first conceived their practical transactions with Captain Cook on the model of sacrifice. Their initial gifts were small pigs, presented as offerings together with the banana plants, sugar cane and ritual formulas suitable on such occasions. Priests took the lead in these prestations at Kauai in 1778. The episode in which the first Hawaiian on board the *Resolution* nonchalantly appropriated what came to hand had been preceded by the proper "orations" chanted at the ship's side. And while the Hawaiians were soon disabused of the idea that they had a right to everything they saw—conduct which, as Cook wrote, "we convinced them they could not persevere in with impunity" (Cook and King 1784 v.2:2105)—later Hawaiian traditions continued to picture their exchange with Cook as offerings of men to god. "They gave him pigs, tapa cloth and all kinds of things in the way one gives things to the god, without demanding a return payment" (Remy 1863:28-29). While this description remained true especially of the Lono priests' relations to Captain Cook at Kealakekua, the commoners and chiefs soon took a different approach. Chiefly transactions with the ships' captains were marked by *noblesse oblige*. Gifts of specially valuable goods, or large amounts of ordinary goods, passed reciprocally between the Hawaiian and European higher instances in the way of disinterested royal transactions. On the other hand, the common people, immediately convinced they could not with impunity take what they wanted, were content to enter into a peaceful commercial exchange of "refreshments" for British iron goods.

But commercial exchange has its own sociology: this is what I mean by "a structure of the conjuncture." Trade does not imply the same solidarities or obligations as communion. On the contrary, trade differentiates the parties to it, defines them in terms of separate and opposed, if also complementary, interests. True that a successful passage of goods will effect a certain concordance between the parties, but the fact remains that the exchange signifies a "between" relation, sociologically distinct from the inclusion implied by Polynesian conceptions of ancestry and sacrifice. Hawaiian men thus passed in practice from one kind of integration with foreigners to another. Their womenfolk were following a similar course, although in a different mode.

From the first days of contact at Kauai, large numbers of ordinary Hawaiian women were insistently demanding sexual relations with the British seamen. They were bent on giving themselves to these beings whom the Hawaiians considered "generally as a race of people superior to themselves." Mr. King, whose conclusion this latter is, also, with many others, testified to the former: to the unequivocal meaning of the gestures of the women who came off to the ships in canoes, expressing "their intentions of gratifying us in all the pleasures the Sex can give" (King Long:20 January 1778). Anxious to prevent the introduction of "the venereal," Cook had published orders at the beginning of both his first and second visits prohibiting his people from having any contact with the local women, whether on ship or on land. The orders were heeded when the sailors found themselves under the eye of their officers, for which the women "abused us (finding nothing could be done by fair words) most sincerely" (Riou Log:28 November 1778). But Cook's tabus could be no proof against the charms and importunities of Hawaiian women, and the corresponding inclinations of the British seamen ("ye inferior people" as Lt. Williamson deemed them). At Kauai, "the Young Women, who were in general exceedingly beautiful, used all their arts to entice our people into their Houses, and finding they were not to be allowed by their blandishments they endeavoured to force them & were so importunate that they would absolutely take no denial . . . it was known that some of those who were on the shore had intercourse with the Women" (Samwell *in* Beaglehole 1967:1083). The same happened at Niihau, and evidently on board the *Discovery* during the first visit.

By the time the British returned, less than a year later, "the venereal" had spread to Maui and Hawaii Island. Finding his best measures and intentions frustrated, Cook finally relented and as of 7 December 1778, while the ships were circumnavigating Hawaii Island, women were permitted on board. The course of true love did not at first run smooth, as it had to cope with the winter swells off Hawaii's northern coast: the women became thoroughly seasick, with results rather disastrous to their paramours (Ellis 1782 v.2:76). But by the time the British reached the south coast, Cook was complaining about the difficulty of working a ship with so many women on board. And at Kealakekua, Samwell would write with his characteristic enthusiasm for the Island women: "We now live in the greatest luxury, and as to the choice of fine women there is hardly one among us that may not vie with the grand Turk himself" (Beaglehole 1967:1159).

I stress that the conduct of the Hawaiian women did not at first merit the title of "prostitution" it was destined to receive. By all accounts their amorous advances were not accompanied by any mercenary stipulations, so far as the British could perceive. "No women I ever met with," Cook wrote, "were less reserved. Indeed, it appeared to me, that they visited us with no other view, than to make a surrender of their persons" (Cook and King 1784 v.2:544). The same tenor appears in the comments of others:

Indeed we found all the Women of these Islands but little influenced by interested motives in their intercourse with us, as they would almost use violence to force you into their Embrace regardless whether we gave them anything or not, and in general they were as fine girls as any we had seen in the south Sea Islands. (Samwell *in* Beaglehole 1967:1085)

There are no people in the world who indulge themselves more in their sexual appetites than these; in fact, they carry it to a most scandalous and shameful degree. . . . The ladies are very lavish of their favours, but are far from being so mercenary as those of the Friendly [Tongan] or Society Islands, and some of their attachments seem purely the effect of affection. (Ellis 1782 v.2:153)

We should also respect the observation made by many of the British that it was the ordinary women, not those of rank, who so offered themselves. But why? Fornander's later apologetics invoke the structure we had considered before, the wife-giving relation between the indigenous people and gods come from Kahiki. "Placed under extremely trying circumstances," he explained, "confronted with men they looked upon as divine, or supernatural beings at least, the Hawaiians gave freely what in their moral ethics there was no prohibition to give; and the seamen—well, they followed the famous saying inaugurated by the Buccaneers and become proverbial ever since, that 'there was no God on this side of Cape Horn' " (1969 v.2:163). The explanation still leaves the behavior undermotivated culturally, but this much seems correctly said: the women gave themselves because they thought there was a god; while the British seamen took them because they had forgotten it.

But there is more: for example, the Hawaiian custom of *wāwāhi* 'to break open'. *Wāwāhi* refers to the offering of virgin daughters to a ranking chief by prominent commoners, a kind of *jus primae noctis,* in the hope of bearing a child by the chief. Such a child would be welcomed by the woman's eventual, regular husband; it would be doubly the first-born, a *punahele* 'favorite child'. For the family then is linked by kinship to the chief, and as Hawaiians say, "The bones of the grandparents will live." An old source cites a prayer accompanying the dedication of a daughter of the people to god by way of consecrating her for a subsequent liaison with the chief:

O the border of the West,
O the firmament above,
O the firmament below,
Here is your treasure.
Devote her to the man that will rule the land,
A husband with an *ahupua'a* [a land district]:
A chief, to preserve your parents,
And your offspring,
To erect a house for you,
A dish-holder for you,
To bake, to fish, to cultivate. . . . (Kekoa 1865)

The mating with the god is, again, an aspect of the complex *'imi haku* 'to find a lord'. In the system of periodic land redistribution, a family without chiefly connections could look forward only to progressive decline in status, property rights and access to wealth. For each new chief put his own people in charge, potentially leaving the favorites of his predecessor to sink into the body of the commonalty. Perhaps the sense of the Hawaiian women's demands on foreign seamen is best represented by an incident that took place when the British left Kauai for the second time, in March 1779, some 13 months after the original visit. A number of men and women came out to the ships in canoes; and while the women remained alongside, the men, following their instructions, went on board and deposited the navel cords of newborn children into cracks of the decks. Commenting on the incident, a modern Hawaiian authority on traditional custom observed: " 'Cook was first thought to be the god Lono, and the ship his "floating island." What woman wouldn't want her baby's *piko* [umbilical cord] there?' " (Pukui et al. 1972:184).

But if for Hawaiian women the giving of their persons to the Europeans was not an ostensibly materialistic proposition, the English seamen knew how to repay the favors granted them. They immediately gave the women's services a tangible value. Again, a structure of conjuncture: they thus defined the relation as a "service." An exchange was instantly begun, from the time Cook relaxed the sexual tabus on 7 December 1778, and the mode of exchange then instituted continued to characterize relations between Hawaiian women and European men well into the nineteenth century. Nor were these the only parties to it. Close male kinsmen of the women would bring them off to the ships, and likewise derive tangible benefits from their sexual commerce. Samwell's description of the first of such transactions with Cook's people epitomizes a good deal of subsequent history:

> They [the Hawaiian women] were very fond of Bracelets which they called Poo-rema [*pu'ulima*], and as we have always made it our study to accommodate our presents to the Taste of the Ladies, we continued to gratify them by stripping our Clothes of Metal Buttons and sewing them on Strips of Red Cloth, which we always found to be very welcome Douceurs to the young women accompanied with a Toi [iron adze] for their Fathers, or whoever brought them on board. (*in* Beaglehole 1967:1152–1153)

Samwell later makes a comment repeated in many European chronicles of subsequent decades (e.g., Nicol 1822:73; Vancouver 1801 v.1:337): "A married man here would as soon let you lie with his wife as his Daughter or Sister, and so long as he got the Toi [adze] into his Possession it was a matter of perfect indifference to him on which of his Family your choice might light" (*in* Beaglehole 1967:1182).

Notice the differentiation of European trade goods into categories of men's things (adzes) and women's (bracelets), and that Hawaiian men gained access to adzes through their women's sexual services, in which they thus acquired a direct economic interest. Cook had a vivid demonstration of the last at Kealakekua—analogous to a celebrated experience of Wallis's at Tahiti—when his seamen began to pry nails from the ships' holds as gifts for their women friends, even as Hawaiian men were using their newly-acquired iron adzes to do the same from the outside, so that between the two they threatened to pull the ships to pieces (Samwell *in* Beaglehole 1967:1164). But this mediation of commoner trade through the women was not one-sided: Hawaiian men, in disposing "provisions" for European goods, began also to demand part of the payment in women's goods, such as bracelets and scissors. "So much were bead bracelets valued at first," Ellis noted, "that a small hatchet and one of these would purchase a hog, which without it could not have been bought for three large hatchets. The women were perpetually teazing the men to dispose of their various articles for these bracelets; at least one of them was always to make a part of the price" (1782 v.2:158). Portlock (1789:159) had the same experience in 1786, as did the Vancouver and later expeditions (Puget Log:21 February 1793; Manby 1929 I(1):14).

Now this economic solidarity between ordinary Hawaiian men and women involved them, at the same time, in a common opposition to their own chiefs. The chiefs had motives as compelling as the women's to act as brokers in the transactions with the foreigners, and even more compelling interests in the foreigners' goods. Moreover, they were given the organizational means and the power to take precedence. This power was partly their own, a condition of their status, and partly developed in the pragmatics of the contact. And the chiefs did not hesitate to unleash the combined effect in untoward violence upon those beneath them.

If the women sought special relations to "ye inferior people" on the European side, the Hawaiian chiefs entered into a privileged alliance with the officers and gentlemen. Here the chiefs' own self-conceptions met a corresponding necessity on the Europeans' part to engage the local power structure in the regulation of trade. "Finding the chief" made eminent political as well as economic sense. Cook, for example, was well aware that unless Hawaiian chiefs could be induced to maintain good order, he would be obliged to use force himself—an alternative that proved true on those occasions when chiefs were absent or lost control of the masses flocking to the ships for trade or other purposes. The moment the *Resolution* sailed into Kealakekua, Cook sought out the men who seemed to command the most authority. The two he found and posted respectively to the *Resolution* and *Discovery* (Kanaina and Palea) proved to be important men in the retinue of the ruling chief, Kalaniopuu. They also proved to be remarkably ready to use force to clear the ships of unwanted numbers of men or women, to punish thieves and to drive off canoes suspected of some undesirable intent. They threw rocks and other projectiles at their countrymen, at times lifted them bodily over the ships' sides, sequestered the property of those detected in theft, pursued and fought with men in canoes who defied their authority and, on one occasion, drowned a man. Mr. Burney summarized the disposition of Palea:

Parreear was always zealous in advising & assisting to punish offenders & several instances happened of his beating them when we excused & let them go, and taking their canoes from them. Indeed on all occasions Parreear was proud of displaying his authority & frequently without much feeling for his countrymen. (Burney Journal:18 January 1779; see Beaglehole 1967:491, 504, 1161, 1164; Cook and King 1784 v.3:157; Law Journal:18, 21, 26 and 27 January *et passim*)

The Kaneoneo incident at Kauai had indeed been paradigmatic. Organized by received categories of Hawaiian culture, the advent of the Europeans nevertheless gave new functional significance to those categories. The forms of chiefly violence upon the underlying population witnessed by the Cook expedition were to be observed repeatedly by later voyages, including the running down of canoes, beatings with sticks and driving off with rocks (e.g., Dixon 1789:125–126; Portlock 1789:155–156; Colnett *Prince of Wales* Journal:2 January 1788; Meares 1790:344–345, 350; Puget Log:21 and 26 February 1793; Bell 1929–1930 I(6):80, 81; Turnbull 1805 v.2:16–19). Not that the chiefs were known to abjure violence in a purely Hawaiian and traditional context. The point is that the traditional context would hardly provide such occasions for it. It did not regularly suppose such competition between chiefs and people over the sources of *mana,* nor otherwise engage the chiefs in such defense of their access to it. But the historic contact with Europeans submitted the relationship between chiefs and people to unparalleled strains. It thus gave this relationship uncustomary functional values.

THE CHIEF'S TRADE AND THE CHIEF'S TABUS

Nor was violence, or the salience of violence, the only novel development in the content of the distinction between chiefs and people. In all the island chiefdoms, the ruling powers-that-be increasingly took preemptory action to insure their disproportionate privileges in foreign trade. On the one hand, they expropriated a goodly share of the common peoples' returns on trade. From the beginning, iron tools and weapons acquired by commoners might be treated something like treasure drifted ashore: traditionally the prerogative of the ruling chief. On occasion, iron goods were seized arbitrarily from commoners' hands; or sometimes such treasure was demanded as an *ho'okupu* 'offering' on the pretext of a ritual collection of the god's due—to the disadvantage, in this case, of the priests as well as the people (Cook and King 1784 v.3:19, 108; Kamakau 1961:98; Dixon 1789:106; Fleurieu 1801 v.2:15; Vancouver 1801 v.3:313; Puget Log:12 and 13 January 1794). It is said that Kamehameha took toll in this way on the returns in specie to the common women's sexual traffic: "It seems that to get money he contrives to exact a kind of tribute from the belles that visit the ship as part of their earnings, while these resort to various contrivances for escaping search" (Iselin n.d.: 79–80). On the other hand, and perhaps more effectively, the chiefs progressively intervened into commoner trade itself, with measures to forestall or engross it on their own behalf, and to make sure it responded to their requirements in foreign goods rather than to those of common people.

The history of the Hawaiian provisioning and sandalwood trades shows the chiefs quick to put regulations on the items most highly valued and heavily demanded by the Europeans. The initial measures include tabus on the commoners' trade in pigs: designed either to prevent such commerce until the ruling chief arrives and disposes of his own produce or to stipulate that pigs be exchanged only for such goods as the chief has need of, such as guns, ammunition, ships' fittings and the like. By 1793–1794, the chiefs' demands for European commodities had markedly differentiated from the peoples' utilities. Iron tools and domestic utensils were no longer of interest to the chiefs; they had a surfeit, even though the people were far from exhausting their own need or capacity for the productive employ of iron. The chiefs' intervention thus had as its object the control of supply from the European side, that it correspond to the exigencies of chiefly power rather than to the peoples' comforts. By the end of Kamehameha's reign, he had set up a system in which ships coming to Hawaii Island, where he was living, could get practically no provisions there. Trade was consistently tabued. The ships were directed on to Oahu or Maui, accompanied by European or Hawaiian agents of the King, where local officials would fill the terms of contracts arranged between the European captain and Kamehameha at Hawaii. Such monopolization of commerce reached a culmination in the sandalwood era, roughly 1804–1828. Trade in sandalwood was a prerogative of the King and such chiefs as he allowed to participate on their own behalf. The labor, of course, was supplied by the people, exacted in the form of a due or rent on land—on pain of dispossession.[11]

For the chiefs, this appropriative relation to trade was a total or cosmological fact: as much "ritual" and "political" as it was "economic." Indeed, by comparison to their European vis-à-vis, for whom political engagements with Hawaiians were organizational means to economic ends, the chiefs found in the commodities of trade more the economic means to political ends. Their own interest in wealth being one of display and consumption rather than production, the chiefs would soon prove unable to compete with enterprising foreigners for Hawaiian lands. Perhaps this also helps explain why they were quick to adapt the power of tabu to the regulation of trade. Yet in thus submitting the concept of tabu to pragmatic improvisations, the Hawaiian rulers went some way toward redefining it. As in many revolutions, the decisive subversion of the system was a work of the people in power: an abuse of power.

It is doubtful that the tabu was, by custom, the *ad hoc* measure of expedience it became in historic times. Even the so-called economic or conservational tabus had a divine finality: they were consecrations of foods to be used in honor of the gods, thus organized in the first place in a system of sacrifice. But then, the ritual power of tabu, the sanctity, encompasses the protection of property, an aspect that may well become dominant in pragmatic structures of trade. (For that matter, human sacrifice in Hawaii underwent the same functional shift: by the end of Kamehameha's reign it appeared as an instrument of criminal justice.) Two passages from Hocart can be used to summarize the transformation:

Thus a traveller sees a reed stuck in the stream, and is told no one may fish there, it is taboo. He inquires no further, because he thinks there is no more in it than that. It is inferred that the taboo is here just a close season, an "economic" taboo. But the river was tabooed, not because fish was getting scarce, but because men who buried the chief had bathed there, or a newborn child's excrements had been thrown into the stream. The taboo would have been imposed whether the fish were scarce or abundant, because the fish were dedicated to the ritual. Pigs and coco-nuts are tabooed because they are required for a feast, and so are holy. (Hocart 1933:189)

Pending systematic work one may suggest that as the ritual is the only effective means of protecting property where there is no organized system of detection, the defence of the 'sacred' rights of property gets concentrated in the hands of the central authority in proportion as the ritual gets so concentrated. This suggestion is not entirely in the air; for we know that Polynesian chiefs used their power of taboo, that is their possession of the word of power, to protect the property of early European explorers by sanctifying it. As the control of the ritual passes out of the hands of the kin into those of the head of the state and his councillors, it is inevitable that everything the ritual is used to effect should also pass into their hands. (Hocart 1933:268)

In the historic period, Hawaiian chiefs did, as Hocart notes, impose tabus to protect the persons and goods of European trade parties on shore. And, with or without priestly collaboration, they also went much further in the pragmatic adaptation of their ritual powers, thus making the sanctity of property a decisive reference of "tabu." Tabus were set to govern, in the chiefs' favor, the rates, times, parties, modes and commodities of the European trade. Occasionally, chiefs would arise above principle to suspend or violate traditionally prescribed tabus, those fixed calendrically for ritual observances, should the interdictions interfere with the observance of critical exchange interests. For eight months of the year, outside the Makahiki season, there were four tabu periods, of two or three days' duration, each lunar month. The chiefs could not then quit the temples, nor was anyone permitted to embark on canoes. The sea was likewise interdicted for extensive intervals of the Makahiki, and again, for all but appropriate fishers, during the 10-day bonito *(aku)*, and mackerel *(opelu)* rituals of January/February and July/August. But European shipping obeyed no such periodicity. It might appear off the coast at any time—even more frequently than usual during the winter Makahiki season. When Vancouver so appeared at the Makahiki of 1794, the famous commander blackmailed Kamehameha into transgression of the annual tabus, forcing him to accompany the British on board from Hilo to Kealakekua, on the threat of doing business instead with the king's archrival Kahekili of Maui (Vancouver 1801 v.5:7–12).

Kamehameha was not pleased with Vancouver's high-handedness.[12] Nor was he—or other high chiefs—often inclined to violate such ritual tabus, however often he improvised "commercial" ones. Kamehameha appears to have had the sense that his capacity to use the tabu pragmatically depended on an adherence to its traditional forms, without which it would lose legitimacy. One reason he retreated to Hawaii Island after 1812 and largely insulated himself and that place from trade, seems to have been the hope of deflecting and confining the contamination to Oahu. The use of resident Europeans as commercial agents would have similar effects. In any event, chiefly violations of ritual tabus in connection with European trade were most frequent during the second decade of the nineteenth century, and at Oahu. Long before that, however, the commoners were defying the dictates of prescribed tabus—and of the chiefs and priests who supported, and were supported by, the concept. Especially were the commoner women flaunting the sacred restrictions.

PRAGMATIC TRANSGRESSIONS AND FUNCTIONAL EFFECTS

Women had been transgressing ritual tabus from the time of Cook's voyage, if not before. I say possibly before, because the tabu did not sit upon Hawaiian women with the force it had for men. The sanction on women's violations, for one thing, was not a susceptibility to sacrifice, as it was for men. The sacrificial offering must be of the nature of the god to whom it is offered, and women as ritually unmarked *(noa)*, descended rather from Earth than the gods, were not suitable as victims (Valeri: n.d.). For the same reason, they were contaminating to everything that had to do with the gods: thus to men themselves when they were under tabu or inherently tabu by status, and to foods that were used in offerings, such as pig, certain turtles, certain bananas and coconuts. Moreover, as men ate in communion with the gods, every meal itself a sacrifice, women could not dine with them, nor could their own food be cooked in the same ovens as men's. Hence the tabu as it affected women was rather the negative image of the consecrated status of men and gods: functioning to protect the sanctity of divine beings and things rather than a positive condition, state or attribute of the women themselves. Nor was it at all certain that an act of transgression on her part would automatically afflict a woman (least of all a chiefly woman, whose status was ambivalent, being tabu as a chief if *noa* as a woman). In historic records, the sanctions of women's tabu violations were socially imposed; they depended on detection and punishment by men, not the malevolent visitation of a god. It is true that such punishments, even unto death, are attested as late as 1817 (Kotzebue 1821 v.2:201); on the other hand, women had also been escaping the effects of their tabu violations since the time of Cook.

The Cook chronicles testify to two sorts of tabu transgressions by ordinary Hawaiian women. First, they ignored interdictions on the sea by swimming out to the ships at night while a tabu was on. On the 29th of January, 1779, Samwell reports, the British ships were put under tabu, and "no Girls were suffered to come on board," presumably because an important chief was scheduled to arrive, and the waters were to be cleared for his advent. In fact, the chief never materialized, but the women did. "These tabus," Samwell comments, "are not so strictly observed but a few Girls can make shift to pay us a visit at night time" (*in* Beaglehole 1967:1171). Secondly, when women slept on board the ships, as on most nights, they did taste of forbidden fruits and pork, and in the company of men—the British seamen. The testimony of Messrs King, Ellis and Samwell is unequivocal on this, if varying in detail regarding the extent of women's transgressions. King writes that they "would eat pork with us in private," though they could not be prevailed upon to touch bananas or turtle (Cook and King 1784 v.3:100).[13] Surgeon Ellis reports:

> The women were not averse to eating with us, though the men were present, and would frequently indulge themselves with pork, plantains and coconuts, when secure from being seen by them. (Ellis 1782 v.2:169)

And Samwell:

> While they ["the Girls"] were on board the ships with us they would never touch any food or ripe plantains except privately & by stealth, but then they would eat very hearty of both & seemed very fond of them. (*in* Beaglehole 1967:1181)

We shall see that both types of violation continued until the tabus were finally abrogated in 1819, as does a third sort, also first documented in 1779: defiance by commoner men of ritual or chiefly prohibitions on the sea or trade. Indeed, there is reason to believe that commoners were transgressing the Makahiki tabus during Cook's entire circumnavigation of Hawaii Island by putting off to trade with the British. Hawaiian traditions of the Cook sojourn say as much, explaining that since Lono was on the water at this time, the people thought they were free to do the same (Remy 1863:26–27). In any event, a clearcut breach of tabu by commoner men is reported for January 1779 at Kealakekua. The Bay had been interdicted the day before in preparation for the arrival of the ruling chief, Kalaniopuu, from Maui. The tabu held on the 24th. But the next morning, the British "endeavoured, both by threats and promises, to induce the natives to come along-side" (Cook and King 1784 v.3:16). The cessation of provisioning was not welcome to Cook's company, and their urging had the desired effect. However, as some canoes were putting off with pigs and vegetable produce, a chief intervened and attempted to drive them back to shore (or, by Mr. Law's version, to run them down). The British thereupon fired some small shot over the chief's canoe, chasing him off. The people's canoes subsequently came out "and refreshments were soon purchased as usual," evidently for the rest of the day (Cook and King 1784 v.3:16). Note the correlation of forces in this incident: a structure of conjuncture in which British power joins with the inclinations of Hawaiian commoners to set the latter against their own chiefs.

Something of the same can be said of Hawaiian women's eating aboard European ships. No doubt they were encouraged by their paramours to thus engage in what one later European visitor called "social living"—by opposition presumably to "natural." Here, in the matter of co-dining and food restrictions on women, was one site in which European and Hawaiian opinions on the culture/nature distinction differed radically. European visitors never ceased to inveigh against the Hawaiian treatment of women—though none, perhaps, with quite the poignancy of Ebenezer Townsend:

> There was one thing very unpleasant to my feelings, who you know, as my mother was a woman, have the highest esteem and respect for the female character, which was to see them all, pleasant, cheerful women, go stooping about decks merely because there happened to be a chief on deck. (1888:73)

Nevertheless, Townsend, along with many other visitors before and after, gave report of how the women continued to set both chiefs and priests at defiance by violating the food tabus: "I found the women very glad to eat of these [forbidden] articles if they were out of reach of detection" (1888:64). That was 1798. A few years earlier, Manby of the Vancouver expedition observed, "When on board the ships a few of them [i.e., the women] would shut themselves up in a cabin and regale most heartily on forbidden eatables'' (1929 I(1):22). So it is noticed in journal after journal, of which Archibald Campbell's observations (1809–1810) are typical:

> Notwithstanding the rigour with which these ceremonies are generally observed [the monthly temple ceremonies], the women very seldom scruple to break them, when it can be done in secret; they often swim off to the ships at night during the tabu; and I have known them to eat the forbidden delicacies of pork and shark's flesh. What would be the consequence of a discovery I know not; but I once saw the queen [Kaahumanu] transgressing in this respect, and was strictly enjoined to secrecy, as she said it was as much as her life was worth. (1819:136)

Likewise, as Campbell says, women broke the ritual tabus that would confine them to shore, sometimes in open disregard of the chiefs or priests. Colnett describes a typical incident at Kauai in 1788: a priest came out to the *Prince of Wales* to call the women on shore because of a "Taboo Boua" (probably *kapu pule,* a monthly tabu ritual); but few of them bothered to obey him (Journal: [no day] February 1788). On a similar occasion in 1793, the women were observed to comply—"our female friends instantly left us"—but not without "many invectives against the barbarous [n.b.] custom that would now confine them to their habitations for two nights and a day" (Manby 1929 I(1):42). Earlier the same month, the women had evaded the interdictions of the bonito tabu by swimming out to Vancouver's ships at night where, says Menzies, "the sailors had the humanity and gallantry to take them in as they came alongside, & in the Society of the honest Tars they found an asylum of freedom more congenial to their disposition & native simplicity" (Menzies Journal:14 February 1793).

As for the disposition of ordinary men to break through the ritual tabus to trade with European ships, it is equally well documented in the post-Cook period:

> Early next morning we had some canoes along-side who brought us water and a few vegetables, notwithstanding the taboo. (Portlock 1789:155)

> All our friends [notably the chiefs and priests] who continued or resided in the neighbourhood [of Kealakekua] were in sacred retirement. This *taboo* was not observed by the lower orders of people with the same degree of strictness as that mentioned in the preceeding chapter [i.e., with regard to the bonito tabu of 1793]. Many of the men were busily engaged in their traffic alongside, but no woman was permitted to be afloat. (Vancouver 1801 v.3:272; Vancouver, however, had noted that one canoe had indeed come off in violation of the bonito tabu, at the hazard of death, 1801 v.3:183–184.)

> And apart from transgressions of ordinary monthly tabu days, the Makahiki tabu or Kamehameha's tabus on trade [cf. Lisiansky 1968 (1814):101–103], there were violations

of the mackerel tabu period, for "although the taboo was very rigidly enforced, their curiosity could not be restrained." (Townsend 1888:57)

The respective relations of chiefs and people to the European presence thus set them in practical opposition to one another. I reiterate that the engagement of different categories of Hawaiian society—women, men and chiefs—to the foreigners from Kahiki was traditionally motivated: the interests they severally displayed in the European shipping followed from their customary relationships to each other and to the world as Hawaiians conceived it. In this sense, Hawaiian culture would reproduce itself as history. Its tendency was to encompass the advent of Europeans within the system as constituted, thus to integrate circumstance as structure and make of the event a version of itself. But in the event, the project of cultural reproduction failed. For again, the pragmatics had its own dynamics: relationships that defeated both intention and convention. The complex of exchanges that developed between Hawaiians and Europeans, the structure of the conjuncture, brought the former into uncharacteristic conditions of internal conflict and contradiction. Their differential connections with Europeans thereby endowed their own relationships to each other with novel functional content. This is structural transformation. The values acquired in practice return to structure as new relationships between its categories.

Ordinary men and women developed a solidary interest in the acquisition of foreign *mana* and domestic utilities distinct from, and opposed to, the chiefly acquisition of power from the same source. The so-called prostitution of Hawaiian women is important here for several reasons: it involved the valorization of a local resource—in considerable demand, besides—other than the agricultural produce, especially pigs, over which chiefs would exert more direct claim and control; the exchange with common seamen bypassed the alliance between Hawaiian and European elites that otherwise regulated commercial intercourse; by its nature, the "service" provided by women called for domestic returns, an exchange moreover that might be relatively concealed from chiefly view. The schismogenic cleavage thus opened between commoners and chiefs became manifest during the earliest encounters with Europeans.

In the days following Cook's murder, while hostilities between the British and Hawaiians were still on, commoner men and women nevertheless secretly maintained their exchange relationships with the British. This at some risk to their own lives and by contrast especially to the suspension of amicable contacts by their own chiefs, from whom the British were attempting by force and negotiation to recover Cook's body. "Notwithstanding our state of hostility," Mr. Trevenan wrote, "the Women swam off to the ships every night. Having the guard about midnight & observing an Indian [i.e., an Hawaiian] jump overboard, I presented my musket & should certainly have fired had I not been luckily told it was a woman" (*in* Beaglehole 1967:559n; cf. King and Samwell to the same effect, *in* Beaglehole 1967:563, 1204). Cook was killed on the 14th of February 1779 and peace with the chiefs was not made until the 22nd. On 17 February, the British set fire to the (innocent) priestly settlement at Kekua, killing several people in the ensuing skirmish. The women on board the British ships thought it all a fine show:

> It is very extraordinary, that, amidst all these disturbances, the women of the island, who were on board, never offered to leave us, nor discovered the smallest apprehensions either for themselves or for their friends ashore. So entirely unconcerned did they appear, that some of them, who were on deck when the town was in flames, seemed to admire the fight, and frequently cried out this was *maitai,* or very fine. (Cook and King 1784 v.3:77)

The translation here is correct, and Samwell, who heard the same on the *Discovery,* adds

> at the same time we could see the Indians flying from their Homes all round the Bay, and carrying their canoes & household goods on their backs up the country. (*in* Beaglehole 1967:1213)

On the 18th of February, under cover of night, a number of common people, as well as priests of Lono, resumed supplying the ships with provisions. The British again found this remarkable, since the chiefs were openly defying and insulting them, but thanks to the people and priests they did not suffer for food through the remainder of the conflict (Cook and King 1794 v.3:78; Clerke *in* Beaglehole 1967:546). Colnett had an analogous experience at Kauai in 1788: a Hawaiian woman who had a "husband" aboard the *Prince of Wales* betrayed a plot of the local chiefs to seize the ship (Colnett Journal: [no day] February 1788).

TABU IN TRANSFORMATION

The full import of such divisions within Hawaiian society cannot be assessed without considering the implications of practice for the concepts of tabu—from which ensue certain implications of the tabu for the concepts of practice. I do not speak of a "reflection" of social relations in ideological terms. "Tabu" is an integral part of the determination of such categories as 'chief', 'commoner', 'men' or 'women'. Constituting the social nature of persons and groups, tabu is itself the principle of these distinctions. For the same reason, tabu is never a simple reflection upon practice: it is *in* the order of practice, as the organization of it. Even if practice, subject as it also is to other considerations (i.e., of this world), escapes the normal order of tabu, it does not thereby escape the tabu system. On the contrary, the meanings of tabu violations follow from the system. In combination, then, with the perturbations introduced by practice, the tabu logic becomes the mechanism of revaluation of persons and objects it had otherwise originally defined. People and things emerge from the practical encounter with novel tabu values, hence novel relations to each other.

I take notice of two structural effects that developed, in the decades following Cook, from violations of the tabus. The first concerns the cleavage among Hawaiians between commoner men and women on one side, their chiefs on the other. The second concerns the cultural and ethnic separation of Hawaiians and Europeans. The commensality of Hawaiian women and European seamen figures decisively in both processes. In both also, the historical changes consequent upon the transgression of the tabus were predicated on the logic of the tabus.

By eating with men—their sailor "husbands"—and of foods reserved to the gods, Hawaiian women violated the sacred restrictions that had defined them as women. At the same time their menfolk acquired a substantial pragmatic interest in these transgressions, even as parallel breaches of tabu by commoner men were of benefit to their women. Developing in this way a collective and negative relation to the tabu, men and women of the underlying population overrode a distinction in ritual value that had differentially linked them to chiefs. For in terms of tabu, men were like chiefs, in opposition to women. As *sacrifiers* of the quotidian domestic cult, even commoner men were positively tabu by relation to women of the house: the latter not simply ritually unmarked or *noa,* but, when menstruating, *haumia* 'defiling' and (negatively) tabu. The consecrated status of men within their own households was thus the domestic equivalent of the status of chiefs relative to commoners as a class. Commoner men were domestic chiefs. Yet all such metaphors entail a difference as well as a resemblance. The domestic cult was in many respects a microcosm of the major temple rituals presided over by high priests and chiefs, but it was also socially disengaged from the latter. The participation of commoner men in the monthly temple ceremonies appears to have been limited. Campbell describes a service of this type at Oahu in 1809 or 1810 with no more than forty men in attendance (1819:128). Corney, many months in Hawaii during 1815 and 1818, came to the conclusion that, "The common people know nothing more about their religion [i.e., the major temple rites] than a stranger who never saw the islands" (1896:101; cf. Whitman ms. to the same effect: "the common people have nothing to do in matters of religion"). Commoners were, as Valeri (n.d.) remarks, at best spectators of the state cult, at worst its victims.

Enter now the pragmatics of trade which, while unifying commoner men and women in unusual fashion and extent, counterpose them to the interests and tabus of the powers-that-be. Running thus in the same direction as the traditional differences in ritual participation—the exclusion of commoners from the temple cult—the pragmatics of trade would break apart the traditional series of proportions, men:women::chiefs:commoners::tabu:*noa*. For everything that sharpens the distinction between chiefs and commoners, or weakens the distinction between men and women, undermines the equivalence of these oppositions—most especially the complicity of men and women in tabu violations, which negates the entire proportional logic. The class distinction between chiefs and the underlying population was this way foregrounded. It became more pertinent and consequential for social action than the tabu distinctions by gender that had before cut across it. Hence it is not simply that values of given relationships—as between men and women, chiefs and common people—were revised. The relationship between such relationships was revised. Structure is revised.

At the level of practice, something of the same sort happened to the initial relations between Hawaiians and Europeans. When sacrifice turned into trade, the *haole* 'foreigners' turned into men. The foreigners were secularized. An ethnic segmentation set in between themselves and the Hawaiians, segmentation that had not attended their first encounters, at least from the Hawaiian perspective. By 1794, Hawaiians were making distinctions among four Western nations: the British, Americans, French and Spanish (cf. Vancouver 1801: v.5:53). These were, moreover, invidious distinctions: "based on experience" one could say, but not on the kind of empiricism usually connoted by that phrase. The British enjoyed a privileged place in the Hawaiian scheme, because the Hawaiians had killed Captain Cook. But then, Cook alone would be exempt from the reduction to human status suffered by his fellow Europeans, including his own countrymen.

The humanization of their European visitors was, again, *sequitur* to an Hawaiian cultural logic. Insofar as the ethnic differentiation proceeded from trade, it was taken in charge, given determinate form, by certain distinctions Hawaiians made among types and ethics of exchange. There is a critical difference in the Hawaiian view between an amical reciprocal sharing, based on need and *aloha* and appropriate among a wide range of kith and kin, and *kū'ai* 'trade', which is actually a form of impoliteness, implying not merely great social distance but a qualitative difference of social kind between the parties who would engage in such transaction (Handy and Pukui 1972: especially p. 191). To this distance of trade must be added the pollution of tabu, the co-dining of Hawaiian women and European men. In the logic of tabu relations, a sacred status is dissolved, even defiled, by contact with persons or things not themselves consecrated. Quondam gods, the Europeans were thus desacralized by a ritually abusive intercourse with what was *noa:* woman. As we shall see, this did not mean the Europeans had lost their *mana.* On the contrary, to defy the tabus and yet live is, by Polynesian conceptions, the sign of extraordinary *mana.* By these same conceptions, however, *mana* is not tabu. "Tabu" is consecrated things, those set aside, hence of the condition Hawaiians call *akua*—which is to say, in reference to specific beings, 'god'.

No longer 'gods', the Europeans became defiling of what is tabu. The gulf that opened between Hawaiians and foreigners—even including that most favored nation, the English—can be assessed by the treatment accorded to Vancouver's expedition in comparison with Cook's. Whereas Cook in 1779 had been ritually adored at the great temple (Hikiau) of Kealakekua, and his men had camped in and about its precincts repairing sails, recuperating from illness and making astronomical observations, when Vancouver arrived at the same place in 1793 he was urgently requested by Kamehameha not to allow his people to enter any Hawaiian temple. The King asked that Vancouver "give the most positive orders that none of our people, on any account whatsoever, should be suffered to enter their morais, or consecrated places, or be permitted to infringe on their rights or sacred privileges" (Vancouver 1801 v.3:222). (The consequences of such profanation were dramatized in 1816, when the infamous Dr. Sheffer, agent of the Russian American Company, entered a temple at Oahu during a monthly tabu; the temple was considered desecrated and had to be burned down [Kotzebue 1821 v.1:304, 334–35].) When Vancouver left Hawaii Island in 1793, King Kamehameha had to go into ceremonial seclusion in order to purify himself, in part because "of his having transgressed the law by living in such social intercourse with us, who had eaten and drunk in the company of women" (Vancouver 1801 v.3:275; cf. Menzies Journal: 8 March 1793; Puget Log: 26 February 1793).

Taken together, the set of transformations mediated by tabu suggests a permanent dialectic of structure and practice. Revised in practice, in relations of the conjuncture, the categories return to the cultural order in altered relationships to each other. But then, responding to structural change in the cultural order, the relations of the conjuncture change from one historical moment to the next. The practice of a second historical moment engages novel interpretations of men and things, predicated not upon the initial status of the categories but on the revaluations they have undergone. At first godly in Hawaiian eyes, Europeans emerge from the earlier contacts secularized. If they eat with women, they are themselves defiled. If the exchange between them and Hawaiians passes from the sacrificial to the commercial, then an *a priori* union is resolved into an opposition of interests—with a corresponding change in the terms of exchange: Hawaiian prices rise.

By the turn of the nineteenth century, even as the numbers of European visitors steadily increased, Hawaiians found themselves at an ever increasing distance, ethnically, ritually and economically all at once, from foreign power. Still, that power had to be appropriated within the Hawaiian order, if at the expense of further transformations of that order.

THE KING'S AFFINES AND THE FINAL CRISIS OF THE TABU SYSTEM

European *mana* was still the decisive fact of Hawaiian life. True, the Europeans as persons had been humanized. But as such, they were put at a distance from Hawaiian humanity: they were British, Americans, and the like. And this merely gave the old problem of their ultra-human powers new dimensions. For Polynesians generally, to live outside the established order, which is to say without tabu, is an ambiguous state. The lawless wanderer is, on one hand, contemptible: without tabu, he is like a dog, Maori say. Yet, on the other hand, like the gods themselves, he is precisely what is beyond the power of society (Johansen 1954). No doubt that Europeans from the 1790s onward were not Hawaiian gods, but the goods and capacities they possessed embodied a *mana* superior to things Hawaiian. On that account, European goods were still Hawaiian necessities, especially for chiefs. The widening gap between Hawaiians and foreigners had to be bridged, as by royal and commercial exchange. There was also, of course, Captain Cook. His apotheosis and the millenial dimensions of the Lono cult appear now in a new light. If the secularization of the Europeans distanced the Hawaiians from the godly power loose upon the land, there remained the divine Cook to mediate between them and it.

On the level of economic practice, certain resident Europeans and Hawaiian chiefs were put in charge of this mediation, as agents and executives of the relations with visiting ships. Their activities, particularly the Hawaiian chiefs', would give the *coup de grace* to the tabu system. Abruptly, so it has seemed to students of Hawaiian history: a whole religion destroyed in a day, the 19th of November 1819, when King Liholiho publicly ate consecrated foods at the same table with chiefly women. A. L. Kroeber made of the act a prime example of "cultural fatigue," on analogy to the sudden disintegration of overstrained metals

(1948:403). Similarly, Handy (n.d.) dubbed the event a "cultural revolution." Of course, from what has been said here, such characterizations do not seem apt. The tabus began to disintegrate in Cook's time, and continued to do so in succeeding years, the process augmenting particularly at Oahu from about 1810. So when the chiefs did finally abrogate the tabus in 1819, and consigned the temple images to the flames, they found many ordinary people ready to join them. Many had already been doing the like for decades.[14]

But who were these chiefs who precipitated the final crisis? To answer, we must go back to another reformulation of the Hawaiian order, developing from the differential relations among the elite to European power. The chiefs who presided over the abrogation of the tabus in 1819 were certain affinal relatives of King Kamehameha, people who from the time of Vancouver, and particularly after 1812, had been delegated to the negotiation of European contact. In contrast to prominent collateral kinsmen of the King, who were excluded from this intercalary role, the affines became what may be called "the party of the Europeans." They were the same who would later join with American missionaries in opposition to King Liholiho and his English connection. By 1822—in what may be the first text written in the Hawaiian language—the leading woman of this group, Kamehameha's widow Kaahumanu, will be described as the "owner" of the lands of the kingdom (*ka mea nona ka 'aina;* see Barrère and Sahlins 1979:25). Kamehameha's collateral relations, on the other hand, were destined to defend, gloriously but in vain, and at the price of their lives, the truly Hawaiian monarchy.

The pragmatic revaluation of categories thus concerns two classes of chiefs: collateral kin of the ruler's own line and allies by marriage, especially relatives of the king's secondary wives (*punalua*). By selectively delegating to the latter the regulation of European contact, while excluding the former, Kamehameha was following, under new circumstances, a conventional political strategy; thus in appearance he reproduced the categorical scheme of the old regime. The strategy was an Hawaiian version of the Machiavellian principle of ruling by servants rather than by barons. This meant empowering people connected by recent or current marriages to the ruling line rather than relying upon the chief's own brothers or near collaterals as executive agents of his authority. Closest to the ruling chief in rank, the cadets were potentially his greatest rivals. The contention between older and younger brothers is a celebrated condition of Hawaiian—indeed Polynesian—myth and practice. It represents in current interpersonal relations the inevitable fate of collateral lines in a system of rank and succession by genealogical priority. The cadets are progressively displaced downward by the growth of the senior line. Increasingly removed in genealogical distance from the main line, they can look forward only to the loss of status and authority. Or else, they can rebel.

The beauty of the affinal strategy was it interposed "younger brothers" who were beholden to the paramount in the place of the younger brothers were were his rivals, without ostensible contradiction to the ideology of seniority. For by the Hawaiian system, the children of a ruler's secondary wives (and of their brothers) would be *kaikaina* 'younger brothers' to his principal son and heir:

> Special care was taken in regard to chiefs of high rank to secure from them noble off-spring by not allowing them to form a first union with a woman of lower rank than themselves. . . . Afterwards, when the couple had begotten children of their own, if a man wished to take another woman—or the woman another man—even though this second partner were not of such choice blood as the first, it was permitted then to do so. And if children were thus begotten they were called *kaikaina,* younger brothers or sisters of the great chief [i.e. of the tabu child born of the first union], and would become the back-bone (*iwi-kua-moo*), executive officers (*ila-muku*) of the chief, the ministers (*kuhina*) of his government. (Malo 1951:54–55)

As Malo says, the affines of the king are his *iwikuamo'o* 'backbone'—a term that connotes 'kinship' was well as 'support'—and his *'ilāmuku*—a term that connotes 'destroyer' as well as 'executor'. Hence they are made the *kuhina* 'ministers' of the chiefdom. A line of chiefs might continue in this service and position for several generations, becoming eventually the reliable *kaukau ali'i* 'lesser chiefs' in charge of the royal household and the king's wealth. (John Papa I'i, a celebrated figure in nineteenth century Hawaii—ending his career as a justice of the Hawaiian Supreme Court—is an instance in point: see his discussion of his genealogical connection to the Hawaii ruling line [I'i 1959:19–20].) With all his guns, ships, lands and stores to take care of, Kamehameha proliferated the cadres of such lesser chiefs during his long reign. This was his so-called commoner policy: his purported disposition to ignore rank in favor of ability in choosing officials. But most significant within the category of 'backbone' were the kin of a ruler's current wives, par-ticularly those of high status in other islands or chiefdoms. Important people in their own right, these allies stood to become great men in their royal in-law's domain—where, however, they would not have direct claim to succeed him. Here they functioned as a buffer to the king's most dangerous rivals, people whose local descent gave them some legitimate pretentions to the succession, as the recurrent legendary theme of usur-pation of an evil ruler by his younger brother also gave them some "legitimate" hopes.

The distinction between a ruler's relatives by marriage and his brother chiefs thus had significant value in the traditional polity. Great respecter of tradition as well as adroit politician, Kamehameha accordingly put his trust in the kinsmen of his favored wife Kaahumanu. Kaahumanu had notable connections to the ruling line of Maui, as well as important Hawaii Island ancestors. But she was not the mother of Kamehameha's heir (except later, by adoption). The woman who bore the heir (Liholiho) was Keopuolani, a person of the highest Hawaii Island descent and tabus. The Kaahumanu group (Kaahumanu *ma*) included her father Keeaumoku, her brothers "George Cox" (Kahekili Keeaumoku) and "John Adams" (Kuakini), and her collateral "brothers" or mother's brother's sons, "Billy Pitt" (Kalaimoku) and Boki (see Figure 1). As 'backbone', these affinal relatives of the King were given critical political and economic offices. They were accorded large tracts of land for their personal use, over which they became *haku'āina* 'lords'; and they ruled sections of the kingdom as territorial chiefs. Late in Kamehameha's reign, Cox governed Maui, Boki governed Oahu, John Adams governed Hawaii and Billy Pitt was the so-called "Prime Minister" of the Islands.

But in history, as by custom, the *kaikaina ponoī* 'true younger brothers' were excluded from main sources of wealth and power. Customarily, at his accession the paramount redistributes the principal land divisions (*moku*) and districts (*ahupua'a*) of the chiefdom among his followers, ideally in proportion to the closeness of their descent to his (Malo 1951:191-192). Malo, the Hawaiian expert on tradition, however, notes an exception: "The larger districts were not generally assigned to the highest chiefs, lest they thus be enabled to rebel against the government" (1951:194). So in history, the share of Oahu that fell to Kamehameha's own (full) younger brother Kealiimaikai was substantially smaller than the lands gained by Kaahumanu. We shall see in a moment that the same was true of Kealiimaikai's share of Hawaii Island relative to the holdings of Kaahumanu's father. The chiefs that emerged wealthy in land from Kamehameha's conquests were more distant kinsmen and supporters, particularly the Kaahumanu group (cf. I'i 1959:69-70).[15]

To appreciate Kamehameha's discriminatory allocation of power, it should also be remarked that the kingship consisted of several different functions, the exercise of which might entail contradictory demands upon the incumbent (cf. Valeri: n.d.). The military exploits that secured the ruler's lands and the victims of his sacrificial cult could involve him in an active relationship to death contaminating to his ritual functions. Likewise, a chief's tabu status was threatened if, like Kamehameha, he lent a stimulus to production that went so far as his own participation in it. Indeed, in the historic period the extension of the king's economic concerns to the regulation of foreign trade could only involve him in the numerous indignities to tabu that attended this commerce. Up until 1812,

FIGURE I

SOME RELATIONS OF KAMEHAMEHA

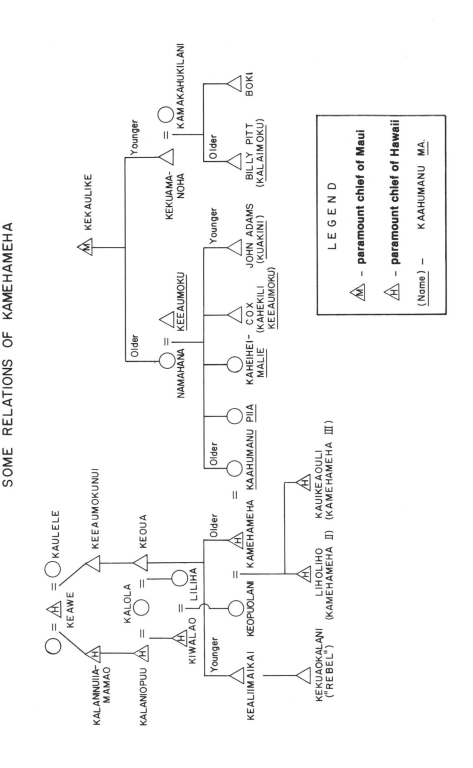

L E G E N D

△ - paramount chief of Maui

△ - paramount chief of Hawaii

(Name) - KAAHUMANU MA.

when he definitively gave up his project of taking Kauai (and Borabora!) by force, Kamehameha was willing to run those risks. He left the care of temple rites to his young heir, Liholiho, while he played the part of "a magnanimous monarch, but a shrewd pork merchant" (Irving 1836:71). When he retreated to Hawaii Island in 1812, however, he gave over active control of trade to supporting chiefs such as Kaahumanu's people. In all this, Kamehameha followed the tradition of royal predecessors, who had likewise variously devised their powers in the ways tactically demanded by reasons of state or by their own tabu rank.

Tactics, however, would have to take account of the structural possibilities of rebellion noted by the Hawaiian sages. This helps explain why the distinction between affinal and collateral relatives of the king is often associated with a difference of, loosely speaking, secular and sacred powers. Devolving "business" as well as territory upon the Kaahumanu group, Kamehameha installed them in the status of *noho hale* occupants of the house, executives of the kingship: a privilege traditionally assigned to *punahele* 'favorites' whose kinship with the ruler was *made* and constituted for them an elevation. Collateral relatives, by contrast, regularly got the care of the ruler's tabus and gods. The legend of Umi is paradigmatic. Umi, the paternal half-brother, whose mother was a countrywoman of lesser rank than the mother of the heir, was given charge of the "kingdom snatching" god (Kukailimoku); whereas, his senior brother inherited the rule (Kamakau 1961:1ff). The same fate was envisioned for Kamehameha, bequeathed the kingdom god by Kalaniopuu, but by most accounts recipient of very little in the ensuing distribution of land, while Kalaniopuu's son (Kiwalao) gained the kingdom itself. Yet the legendary and historical stories of Umi and Kamehameha respectively are paradigmatic also in another way. Holders of the conquering god, thus providers of human sacrifices, both rebelled against their senior brother and seized the government. Another structure of the long run: the son of Kamehameha's younger brother Kealiimaikai, inheritor of the self-same god, likewise attempted to duplicate the rebellious feat in 1819—though under different circumstances and with disastrous consequences. Meanwhile, during Kamehameha's reign, Kealiimaikai was the sometime guardian in his own person of the ruler's tabus, thus freeing his older brother for active (and potentially defiling) tasks of state:

When it came to the building of [the temple] Pu'u-kohola' no one, not even a tabu chief, was excused from the work of carrying stone. Kamehameha himself laboured with the rest. The only exception was the high tabu chief Ke-ali'i-maika'i [Kamehameha's younger brother]. It is said that when this chief saw Kamehameha carrying a stone, he too lifted a stone and started to carry it on his back to Pu'u-kohola'; but when Kamehameha saw him packing the stone on his back he ran and took it away saying,

"You stop that! You must preserve our tabu. I will do the carrying!" Then he ordered Ka-pa'a-lani and some others to take that rock out to mid-ocean so far that land was no longer visible and throw it overboard. Kamehameha certainly thought a great deal of his brother. (Kamakau 1961:154–155)

What Kamehameha thought of, and gave to, his brother by comparison to his allies by marriage is quite evident in the transactions of the Vancouver expedition. The affinal/collateral contrast is here at work in the negotiation of European power—thus foreshadowing the political organization of the events of 1819. Vancouver was puzzled to find that although Kamehameha was then at war with the chief of Maui, he placed extraordinary reliance on "Maui chiefs" resident on Hawaii. They were Kaahumanu's kinsmen. That Kamehameha's in-laws were known as "Maui chiefs," although they also had Hawaii Island descent, seems a significant representation of their distinction from Kamehameha's collaterals, clearly Hawaiian chiefs themselves. The representation is supported by other evidence, such as the interest displayed by Kaahumanu's father (Keeaumoku) in taking the rule of Maui during negotiations with Vancouver over the Cession of Hawaii; or, again, Hiram Bingham's classification of these people in the family of the Maui ruler Kekaulike, by contrast to Kamehameha and Kalaniopuu, which presumably reflects Hawaiian conceptions (Bingham 1969 [1855]:80). Vancouver had been struck particularly by the behavior of two of the "Maui chiefs" assigned by Kamehameha to watch over the astronomical observatory the English established on shore: one the future "Billy Pitt" (Kalaimoku), the other a brother of Kaahumanu who died soon after:

They had been constantly with [the astronomer] Mr. Whidby in the marquee, and *had acquired such a taste for our mode of living, that their utmost endeavours were expended to imitate our ways.* . . . Their attachment was by no means of a childish nature, or arising from novelty, it was the effect of reflection; and a consciousness of their own comparative inferiority. This directed their minds to the acquisition of useful instruction, from those they considered infinitely their superiors. Their conversation had always for its object useful information, not frivolous inquiry . . . and the pains they took to become acquainted with our language, and to be instructed in reading and writing, bespoke them to have not only a genius to acquire, but abilities to profit by instruction. (Vancouver 1801 v.3:270–271; emphasis mine)

These "Maui chiefs," middlemen in the appropriation of European power and disposed to such an interest in it, were also destined to inherit it. But consider the notices in the Vancouver documents of Kamehameha's brother Kealiimaikai. As junior brother, he had been attached in 1793 to the junior ship, the *Chatham* commanded by Puget, from which however he was absent for many days. He finally returned from up-country with a present for Puget of 10 pigs and a large quantity of vegetable provisions. Pigs were the principal item of exchange with Europeans, but from all contemporary accounts this modest gift of Kealiimaikai's was only about one-fourth or one-fifth the number of pigs presented to the ships by Kaahumanu's father. Still, it was all Kealiimaikai could do, since, in conformity with political principle, the dangerous younger brother had been allowed only limited resources:

> This [present] I was given to understand by Davis [an important English advisor of Kamehameha] was absolutely as much as Kealiimaikai would well afford, he being kept in a continued state of indigence, though first brother to Kamehameha, to prevent his being troublesome or by an accumulation of riches, he might encourage rebellious factions to overthrow the present King, who only held the sceptre by usurpation. (Puget Log:24 February 1793)

Nor was Kealiimaikai one of the chiefs of the six divisions (*moku*) who formally ratified the Cession of Hawaii Island to Vancouver in 1794. Kealiimaikai was present on the occasion, as were two other (half) brothers of Kamehameha, but except for an insignificant district given to one of the half brothers, they were excluded from ruling (Bell 1929–1930 II(2):127; Vancouver 1801 v.5:90–91). On the other hand, Keeaumoku was also there, as was his daughter Kaahumanu, Keeaumoku governing the rich and pivotal division of Kona.

The Kaahumanu *ma* not only went on to rule the unified kingdom of Hawaii, they did so by the techniques and means of European power they had so well studied and made their own. Managers of European trade, owners of ships and stores of property purchased in their own right, they were, as I say, the party of the *haole* 'white men'. Under their particular sponsorship and urging, the tabus were abolished upon the death of Kamehameha and investiture of Liholiho. I will not rehearse here the incidents of the events of 1819, but merely take note of the part played by Kaahumanu and her people—by comparison with Kekuaokalani, the son of Kamehameha's brother Kealiimaikai.[16]

In the years immediately preceding the cultural "revolution" of 1819, many chiefs, as well as common people, held the tabus in contempt. There is plenty of retrospective testimony to this effect from the 1820s, mainly from missionaries, but some also from contemporary accounts of explorers or merchants. Golovnin wrote, as of 1818:

> Elliot [Juan Elliot d'Castro, Kamehameha's English-Portuguese "physician," on and off the Islands since 1814] told me that the more important the chief, the less he observes these regulations, and that these free-thinkers, so to speak, are more friendly to Europeans and get along with them much better. (Golovnin 1979:209)[17]

Among the chiefs "more friendly to Europeans," the ones we can positively identify as "free thinkers" were Kaahumanu's brothers. Indeed, Billy Pitt and Boki had themselves baptized as Catholics by Freycinet's chaplain aboard the *Uranie* in August, 1819. As for Cox, Peter Corney, in the Islands on several occasions from 1815–1818, had this to say:

> I have frequently questioned the chiefs about their religion, and their general answer was, that they go to the Morais [the temples] more to feast than to pray, which I believe really to be the case. Mr. Cox or Teymotoo, that I have before mentioned, sets the wooden gods and priests at defiance; he says, that they are all liars, and that the white man's God is the true and only God. (Corney 1896:102; n.b., the first Christian missionaries arrived in 1820.)

Kamehameha was well aware of this attitude, shared of course by European visitors as well as certain of his chiefs, but he held out against it. "These are our gods, whom I worship," he told Kotzebue in 1816, "whether I do right or wrong, I do not know; but I follow my faith, which cannot be wicked, as it commands me never to do wrong" (1821 v.1:312). When Kamehameha died (8 May 1819), however, he effectively left his free-thinking Maui allies in power. Kaahumanu, indeed, presided over the installation of Liholiho as Kamehameha II some days later, taking the occasion to pronounce before the assembled Hawaiian notables the purported will of the deceased King that she rule jointly with his heir. Kaahumanu also seized the opportunity to proclaim that those who wished to follow the old tabus might do so,

> but as for me and my people [i.e., the Maui "backbone"], we intend to be free from the tabus. We intend that the husband's food and the wife's food shall be cooked in the same oven, and that they shall eat out of the same calabash. We intend to eat pork and bananas and coconuts [sacrificial foods prohibited to women], and *to live as the white people do*. (Alexander 1917:40; emphasis added)

Recall Vancouver's prophetic words about Kaahumanu's "people": that they had "acquired such a taste for our own mode of living." But if these affinal kinsmen figured their existence henceforth as European rulers, certain collateral relatives of the dead King, excluded from the management of foreign power, would be the party of the Hawaiians. They would defend Hawaiian culture. For they had inherited the Hawaiian gods. Just as Kealiimaikai, the younger brother, had been assigned the care of the King's personal tabus, so Kamehameha bequeathed upon Kealiimaikai's son Kekuaokalani the charge of his personal and sacrificial god, *Kukailimoku*. As in the legend of Umi and the biography of Kamehameha, Kekuaokalani took his legacy as a right of rebellion, defying the new king and the "free eaters," and rallying many to his cause. But in this case, he did not claim the rule simply in pursuit of personal ambition or by virtue of the *'ino* 'wickedness' of the reigning chief. He claimed it for the Hawaiians, as against the Europeans and their chiefly compradors.

Freycinet visited Hawaii in August, 1819, in the midst of the turmoil. From John Young, the most important and informed of Kamehameha's English chiefs, he got an account of the rebel Kekuaokalani's program:

> he proposed no less than the overthrow of the royal power and the massacre of all the Europeans settled in the Sandwich Islands. They were the ones, according to him, that had contributed the most to bring them under subjection, and to bring about the concentration of power in the hands of one person. . . . war was anticipated. (Freycinet 1978:20)

Freycinet also heard of Liholiho's economic concessions to the chiefs who supported him, Kaahumanu's people notably. They were to be given free right to cut sandalwood from their extensive domains, and trade it on their own behalf, ending the King's monopoly regulations.

Meanwhile, Kekuaokalani owned the King's god. But it was a weakened god. Human sacrifice had been declining in frequency through the first two decades of the century (Shaler 1808:167; Corney 1896:102; Chamisso *in* Kotzebue 1821 v.3:247–248). There is a suggestion in Hawaiian tradition that Kekuaokalani revived it; if so, it would constitute a preemptory claim to rule.[18] At the same time, Liholiho was demonstrating his own spiritual disqualification for power: twice he failed to properly perform temple rites, because he was drunk (Lahainaluna [Anonymous]). But if Kekuaokalani held the god, Liholiho in October joined his chiefly supporters in proclaiming there were no gods anyway. And how many bayonets had the pope's divisions? The affinal Maui chiefs controlling the King and Kingdom also controlled the greatly superior royal stores of guns and ammunition that they had been instrumental in accumulating. In December 1819, Kekuaokalani was killed in a battle with the anti-tabu forces commanded by Billy Pitt.[19]

THE "NEW" ORDER

In the sequel there would be another significant change, although perhaps better considered a permutation than a transformation, since the structure was preserved in an inversion of its values. Descendant of voyagers from Kahiki, the traditional Hawaiian chief had been identified with the ultrahuman powers of distant places and original times. By tradition also, the immigrant chiefly line appropriated Hawaiian powers by marriage and with a native-born chiefess. The 'indigenous' or 'true' chiefs—the same word, *maoli,* does for both—were wife-givers to "the shark that travels on land." But by 1819, the system had, as it were, reverted to an earlier state. For the true *Hawaiian* chiefship, as represented by Kekuaokalani, was now defined as indigenous and opposed to an essentially foreign *mana* i.e., to the power detained by the Kaahumanu crowd, who intended "to live as the white men do." Thus now it was the wife-givers, traditionally the native victims of a foreign usurpation, who ruled by external means. Moreover, these maternal kinsmen of the new King, specifically Kaahumanu, assumed a ritual role from which they were excluded by custom. Now it was they who regulated worship.

Even the abrogation of the tabus was a ritual act—as tabu-removal always is in Polynesia. The high priest Hewahewa and the tabu chiefess Keopuolani also figured prominently in the affair, and the event appears in later historical documents as "the time they tabued the temples." But within a few years, the Kaahumanu group would honor precedent by restoring the tabus. Only this time the tabus at issue were the uncompromising restrictions of a fanatical Calvinism, whose head missionary, the American Hiram Bingham, was explicitly considered by Kaahumanu and her brothers as their own *kahuna nui* 'high priest'. The conversion notably took effect after Liholiho's death in England in 1824.

Thus a structure of the long run shadows forth in the historic change. The entire episode of tabu abolition can be seen as a prolongation of the death ceremonies of Kamehameha. Normally at the death of a ruler the tabus were suspended: free-eating and various forms of ritual inversion took place for a ten day period, including fornication between high-born women and low-born men, after which the heir returned from seclusion and with his accession restored the tabus. At Liholiho's installation, Kaahumanu had simply tried to prolong the ritual license; indeed the feast of 19 October 1819 which brought success to the attempt was a memorial rite of Kamehameha's death (cf. Davenport 1969). Five years later, shortly upon receiving news of Liholiho's death, Kaahumanu abruptly turned pious—the "new Kaahumanu" the missionaries called her—and reinstated the reign of tabu.

Liholiho was succeeded by his younger brother, Kauikeaouli, who took office as Kamehameha III. But the new King, as his older brother—if quite unlike their royal forebears—now stood for the Hawaiian concept of *haunaele* 'disorder', in opposition to the Christianized chiefs and their missionary priests. The missionaries called the King's proclivities "backsliding." It was both a personal disorderliness, manifested in royal bouts of inebriation, and complicity or leadership in a series of rebellions, in 1829, 1831 and 1833–1834, aimed at restoring the powers of the throne. In these revolts, the King would proclaim a state of *noa*, abrogation of the (Christian) tabus, and demonstrate against the missionaries' and chiefs' rules by sponsoring drunken and licentious revels, prominently featuring the revival of Hawaiian *hula* dancing. At the failure of one of these attempts at political and cultural restoration, a supporter of the King was heard to lament, "the Hawaiian gods were silent and could do no harm" (Reynolds Journal: 5 March 1831).

Thus the set of inversions that, by *mauvaise foi,* nevertheless kept faith with the old system. Originally foreign, the King now appears as the native Hawaiian. The one who customarily placed the tabus at his accession, he would now throw them off. Kaahumanu's people, by category wife-givers and deposed native chiefs, seize power by virtue of their access to foreign resources. And the woman reestablishes the tabu order. Thus king and affines, men and women, foreign and indigenous, tabu and *noa* all exchanged their places. Even more, after the first two rebellions of the King's party had been suppressed, Kaahumanu imitated the ancient rites of chiefly confirmation in a perverse form by circuiting the islands in clockwise direction, proclaiming the Christian tabus and building new churches as she went. So had the traditional paramount chief legitimated his succession by consecrating the temples (*luakini*—the same word was used for Christian churches) in a tour of his domain. King Kauikeaouli's own last act of defiance was to circle Oahu himself in 1834. At the end of the circuit—taken, however, in the ritually sinister direction, counter-clockwise—he made the consummate royal gesture, traditionally symbolic of a refusal to share power, by publicly fornicating with his sister before the assembled Christian chiefs. Next day he attempted suicide. Comments a missionary journal of the time, "There is indeed wickedness in high places!" (Chamberlain Journal: 22 July 1834).

4 Conclusion
Structure in History

Basically, the idea is very simple. People act upon circumstances according to their own cultural presuppositions, the socially given categories of persons and things. As Durkheim said, the universe does not exist for people except as it is thought. On the other hand, it need not exist in the way they think. Nor need the response of the "generalized other" of human discourse, having also his or her own cultural standpoint, correspond to the suppositions of one's own intentions and conceptions. In general, then, the worldly circumstances of human action are under no inevitable obligation to conform to the categories by which certain people perceive them. In the event they do not, the received categories are potentially revalued in practice, functionally redefined. According to the place of the received category in the cultural system as constituted, and the interests that have been affected, the system itself is more or less altered. At the extreme, what began as reproduction ends as transformation.

"Reproduction" has become a fashionable term these days, rather taking the theoretical place of, or specifying, the notion of "function." But one may question whether the continuity of a system ever occurs without its alteration, or alteration without continuity. Even the apparently extreme processes of culture-in-history we have been discussing, reproduction and transformation, are they truly—i.e., phenomenally—distinct? Clearly, they are analytically separable. On one hand, contexts of practical action are resumed by a conventional wisdom, by already given concepts of actors, things and their relations. Thus was Cook, from the Hawaiian view, the returned god Lono. And this was surely reproduction. On the other hand, the specificity of practical circumstances, people's differential relations to them, and the set of particular arrangements that ensue (structure of the conjuncture), sediment new functional values on old categories. These new values are likewise resumed within the cultural structure, as Hawaiians incorporated breaches of tabu by the logic of tabu. But the structure is then transformed. Here the cultural encompassment of the event is at once conservative and innovative. It would seem that a good Heraclitean argument can be made for the inseparability of continuity and difference (Wagner 1975). At the least, all structural transformation involves structural reproduction, if not also the other way around.

I argue too that such effects as transformation and reproduction are maximally distinguishable in situations of culture contact, although the processes involved are by no means unique to these situations. For here, in the clash of cultural understandings and interests, both change and resistance to change are themselves historic issues. People are criticizing each other. Besides, their different interpretations of the same events also criticize each other, and so allow us a proper sense of the cultural relativity of the event and the responses to it. Still, all these processes are occurring in the same general way within any society, independently of radical differences in culture, so long as actors with partially distinct concepts and projects relate their actions to each other—and to a world that may prove refractory to the understandings of any and all concerned.

INTEREST AND VALUE

But there is more to our scheme than the other's or the world's resentments. Any comprehension of history as meaning must recognize the distinctive role of the sign in action, as opposed to its position in structure. Action, we say, is intentional: guided by the purposes of the acting subject, his or her social living in the world. Engaged thus in life projects, the signs by which people act are brought into referential relation to the objects of their actions, thus giving particular contextual meanings to the conceptual values. Again in action, signs are subject to contingent arrangements and rearrangements, instrumental relations that also potentially affect their semantic values. All such inflections of meaning depend on the actor's experience of the sign as an *interest:* its place in an oriented scheme of means and ends.

The word "interest" derives from a Latin impersonal verbal expression meaning 'it makes a difference'. An interest in something is the difference it makes for someone. Happy etymology, since it runs parallel to the Saussurean definition of the conceptual value of the sign. The sign is determined as a concept by its differential relation to other signs in the collective symbolic scheme. On the other hand, the sign represents a differential interest to various subjects according to its place in their specific life schemes. "Interest" and "sense" (or "meaning") are two sides of the same thing, the sign, as related respectively to persons and to other signs. *Yet my interest in something is not the same as its sense.*

Saussure's celebrated discussion of linguistic value helps make the point, as it is framed on an analogy to economic value. The value of a five-franc piece is determined by the dissimilar objects with which it can be exchanged, such as so much bread or milk, and by other similar units of currency with which it can be contrastively compared—one franc, ten francs, and the like. By such relationships the significance of five francs in the society is constituted. Yet this general and abstract social sense is not the value of five francs *to me*. To me, it appears as a particular interest or instrumental value, and whether I exchange it for milk or bread, give it away or put it in the bank, all depends on my particular circumstances and objectives. As implemented by the historic subject, the conventional value of the sign acquires an intentional value, and the conceptual sense an actionable reference.

I do not say that interest derives from "the individual" in contradistinction to "the social." Interest is a social fact, and the individual is a social being. The fact would still be social even if it were unique to some individual, just as the individual—precisely in his or her capacity as a social being—has a situation and experience not the same as anyone else. What is at issue here is the difference between the enactment of the sign by the subject and its constitution in the society. As an interest, the sign does not even present itself to consciousness in the same way it is socially constituted as a sense. Buying filet mignon for dinner rather than hamburger in order to celebrate an important occasion or entertain a distinguished guest appears to (American) people merely as right and proper. The interest they have in steak as a socially instrumental value, this subjective experience of steak, is of different order than the process by which steak is constituted as a differential or positional meaning in the total system of foods. The intentional value of course derives from the conventional value—also, in history, vice versa—but the latter is an intersubjective relationship of signs, different in quality and mode of existence from personal experience.

We can say that as lived and acted upon, the symbolic fact is a phenomenal "token" whose "type" is its mode of existence in the culture-as-constituted. Now in the culture-as-constituted the sign has an abstract sense, merely signifying, by virtue of all possible relations with other signs, all its possible occurrences: it is "stimulus free," not bound to any particular worldly referent. But people live in the world as well as by signs, or better, they live in the world by signs, and in action they index the conceptual sense by reference to the perceived objects of their existence. In naive and evidently universal human experience, signs are the names of things "out there." What I am trying to say in a too fancy way was more simply put by an Indian recounting his experiences with the Canadian government in Ottawa: " 'An ordinary Indian can never see the "government." He is sent from one office to another, is introduced to this man and to that, each of whom sometimes claims to be the "boss," but he never sees the real government, who keeps himself hidden' " (cited for a different, but related, purpose in Lévi-Strauss 1966:239n).

THE TRANSFORMATION OF CONCEPTUAL VALUES

In action then, and in their capacity as interests, signs can acquire new conceptual values: (1) insofar as they are placed in novel relationships with objects in the referential process; and, (2) insofar as they are placed in novel relationships with other signs in the instrumental process. Reference is a dialectic between the conceptual polysemy of the sign and its indexical connection to a specific context. Notoriously, signs have multiple meanings as conceptual values, but in human practice they find determinate representations, amounting to some selection or inflection of the conceptional sense. And because the "objective" world to which they are applied has its own refractory characteristics and dynamics, the signs, and by derivation the people who live by them, may then be categorically revalued.

I stress the word "revalued" because the referential determination of the sign is not a simple expression of the "true" nature of things, as a naive empiricism might suppose. Reference is always a symbolic reference. For the world is experienced as already segmented by relative principles of significance; and even if the experience proves contradictory to people's categorical presuppositions, still the process of redefinition is motivated in the logic of their cultural categories. The innovative value is still a relationship between signs and cannot be determined directly from the "objective" properties of the referents. If Hawaiians decided the British were not gods because the seamen insisted on eating with women, the conclusion was no simple *sequitur* to the empirical fact of commensality. It followed, rather, from an elaborate logic of tabu and cosmic determinations of the meaning of men and women. Nothing in the act of eating with someone proves you are not really a god. When European officers and sailors ate with Hawaiian men it had no such effect on their status—Hawaiian men always eat in the presence of the gods.

All "copy" theories of the relations between meanings and things can thus be put aside. But it would still remain that the indexical referencing of signs in the course of action can influence their conceptual values. When Hawaiian chiefs, in the interest of engrossing trade, employed the concept of tabu in an *ad hoc* and expedient way, it at least rendered one of the possible uses of that concept more salient than it had been traditionally. The action reordered the semantic field of "tabu." Indeed, the absence of a definite ritual finality, coupled to the presence of a (culturally) determinate material interest, shifted the meaning of tabu toward a dominant sense of legal interdiction, as in a proprietary right. In Hawaii today, if one sees a sign reading KAPU on a fence, it means 'no trespassing', and the sanction behind it is somewhat different than that of the gods.

The same example can illustrate the effect of instrumental rearrangements of signs in the course of human action. In structure or culture-as-constituted signs are in a state of mutual determination. They are defined as "coordinated with, not subordinated to one another, not in one direction only as a series, but reciprocally as in an aggregate." God the Father is understood by relation to God the Son, and vice versa: the significance of a given symbolic form depends on the co-presence of the others. But action unfolds as a temporal process. And here the value of any given sign, as an instrumental value for a given subject, depends precisely on the subordination of one sign to another "in one direction only." In action, the logic of relationships between signs lies precisely in their orientation: sequentially and consequentially, as means and ends of people's purposes. People, moreover, are constantly putting signs in various and contingent relationships. I can use my five francs to buy any one of a number of goods, or as a gift to a kinsmen or a bribe to an official, to pay a debt or to throw in a well and make a wish. The Hawaiian chiefs, for good and traditional reasons, consistently used the power of tabu in an unprecedented manner to accumulate property in trade. Doing so, they functionally displaced the received relationships of the concept, away from the supernatural and the ritual, toward the material and the political. Such action thus effected new positional relationships among categories of the system, which is to say a novel set of reciprocal delimitations of the elements—or, in short, a different structural state.

Once again, there is no need to fall into a naive utilitarianism. We know that the chiefs' relations to trade goods developed from a relative, Polynesian scheme of meanings: their economic rationality was neither eternal nor even particularly "economical" by European standards. Moreover, Hawaiian history shows that whether or not, or to what extent, a subjective revaluation of signs will have structural effect depends on many conditions of the culture-as-constituted: the improvisations that can be logically motivated, as by analogy, metaphor or other tropes; the institutional freedom to do so; the place of the actor in a social hierarchy that gives his or her action structural weight, makes it more or less consequential for others. The example of Hawaiian chiefs and the tabus also shows, by comparison to the effects of commoners' transgressions, that a privileged position in the culture-as-constituted may amplify the consequences of an individual's action. In any case, action begins and ends in structure: begins in the projects of people as social beings, to end by absorption of the effects in a cultural practico-inert. Yet in the interim the categories may be functionally displaced, their respective positional values altered; hence, by definition, a new structural order is in place.

The person, action in the world, the revaluation of the sign in practice and the return to structure: all of this still has too much of an air of solipsism, as if everything came down to the individual in isolation, in the manner of an economic argument from Robinson Crusoe. Nor is it enough to specify that this individual is not squatting outside the universe, that he is a social subject through and through. We must bring into account the relations of practice itself, the "structure of the conjuncture." My argument has been that there is a *sui generis* development of cultural relationships at this level: a working-out of the categories of being and things as guided by interests and fitted to contexts. We have seen that such "working disagreements"—to borrow a phrase the Bohannans use in an analogous context—may entail some arrangement of conflicting intentions and interpretations, even as the meaningful relationships so established conflict with established relationships. Hawaiian sacrifice to the gods turned into commercial exchange with the Europeans. But Hawaiian men participated in the exchange on a different footing than women, as did chiefs than commoners in general, priests than chiefs, not to mention pigs than dogs, yams than taro or Oahu than Maui. In this structure *of* practice, then, relationships themselves are put at issue, not just this or that cultural category. The differential integration of men and women or chiefs and commoners with European power affected their perceptions of, and conduct toward, each other. This, I would stress, is what makes transformation really radical: something more than an alteration of contents or a permutation of values, the system otherwise remaining the same.

The dialectics of history, then, are structural throughout. Powered by disconformities between conventional values and intentional values, between intersubjective meanings and subjective interests, between symbolic sense and symbolic reference, the historical process unfolds as a continuous and reciprocal movement between the practice of the structure and the structure of the practice.

Notes

[1] Glottal stops are not indicated for proper names throughout this essay, due to their absence in many sources and lack of agreement between sources. Common Hawaiian terms, however, are diacritically marked following Pukui and Elbert (1965).

[2] It is often claimed that Vancouver had an extraordinary influence on Kamehameha, and thereby on the political system set in place by the latter (e.g., Kelly 1967). To the extent this is true—though I think it exaggerated—it is consistent with the thesis developed here concerning the consequences of Cook's death and power given the English by virtue of the place assumed by Cook in the Hawaiian pantheon. The same seems involved in the tradition preserved by Hawaiians to the effect that Vancouver had promised to send them missionaries. Vancouver's relation to Hawaiian religion was not simple. On the one hand, he once obliged Kamehameha to break an important tabu for the convenience of the British. On the other hand, he complied with Kamehameha's request that the British keep out of Hawaiian temples. He also had his ships observe a Hawaiian lunar tabu period (*kapu lā* or *kapu pule*). And in the terms of the Cessation of Hawaii Island, he specified that the Hawaiian religion was not affected by the treaty and would be respected. No doubt many of Vancouver's people, as Europeans before and after them, chided the Hawaiians on their religious beliefs and practices. As we shall see, Kamehameha typically responded to such criticisms by acknowledging that what the European said might be true, but his gods had been good to him, and he intended to stick by them.

[3] Lono is a classical Frazerian deposed god/king. Analogous myths and ceremonies are widespread in Polynesia and beyond; the *milamala* of the Trobriands, involving the return of the clan dead (*baloma*) is a variant. The deposition of Lono in Hawaiian folklore is figured more particularly in legends of certain chiefs, as befits the "epic" rather than "mythic" character of this folklore (see Beckwith 1972). A classic mythical form of the same theory was described for the gods Tangaroa and Rongo of Mangaia by Gill, Tangaroa here being the older and deposed brother, whose annual return is signified by the fruiting of the breadfruit tree (Gill 1876).

[4] The designation of Cook as Lono ("Orono," "Erono," etc.) does not appear in the transactions of the visit to Kauai in 1778, although Cook received the prostration appropriate to divine chiefs when he first went ashore. King's footnote (Cook and King 1784 v.3:5n) regarding "Orono"—"Captain Cook generally went by this name amongst the natives of Owhyhee"—seems conclusive, since "Owhyhee" refers at this period to Hawaii Island, the entire group being known to the British as the Sandwich Islands.

[5] I should stress the interpretative character of certain of my remarks on the gods' circuit and the *kāli'i* ritual. The identification of the short god (*akua poko*) with the king is particularly motivated by the observation of John Papa I'i (1959:75–76) that in the early nineteenth century Makahiki ceremonies on Oahu, the short god traveled to Kailua and Kaneohe. These were Kamehameha's own lands. It is also likely that at an earlier period the god-images of each division (*moku*) chief on Hawaii Island similarly made a left and inland circuit within the division. Regarding the *kāli'i,* it is well testified for early historical times that Kamehameha took pride in successfully parrying all the spears thrown at him on such occasions; he also dispensed with the expert spear-dodger who precedes the king at the

Makahiki to ward off the first spear (Corney 1896:101–102; Lisiansky 1814:119). Since both Malo (1951:150) and K. Kamakau (*in* Fornander 1916–1919 v.6:144) specify that the king is touched by the second spear at the Makahiki, it is possible that Kamehameha had introduced a change in the traditional rite. Whether by tradition the king ritually died when he came ashore or regained the kingdom (or both) does not affect the general point made here that the land falls to Lono during the circuit of the Makahiki image; whereas, the King has retaken possession by the time the image is dismantled, Lono's gift of abundance has been shaken to earth and the "canoe of Lono" sent back to Kahiki. See also Daws (1969a) who diagnoses the opposition of Ku and Lono during the Makahiki, although he appears to misplace the timing and significance of the *kāli'i* in relation to Cook's death. In 1779 the *kāli'i* took place on 4 January rather than on 11 February as Daws suggests.

[6] I am most grateful to Ms. Jocelyn Linnekin and Mr. William Fay for working up the computer program and printout of the correspondence between European dates and lunar phases. In an appendix to a forthcoming publication (*The Dying God or the History of the Sandwich Islands as Culture*) I present a day-by-day tabulation of the historical events of the Cook voyage alongside the corresponding daily observances of the Makahiki. The principal accounts of the Cook voyage are: Beaglehole (1967), which includes, besides Cook's own journal, the journal of David Samwell and excerpts of Clerke's and King's records, as well as references (in footnote) to various other logs and proceedings; the "official" publication of the voyage (Cook and King 1784); and the published works of Ellis (1782), Zimmermann (1930) and Rickman (1781). Important unpublished logs or journals which I also draw upon here include those of Riou, Law, Gilbert, Edgar and Burney (see References).

[7] Cook and the Hawaiian king were rivals in exactly the same way as Cortés and Montezuma: the former the returning, ancient non-sacrificial god (Quetzelcoatl), the latter associated with the imperial and sacrificial god (Huitzilipochtli).

[8] By all evidence, it appears that an explicit myth of the annual return of Lono from Kahiki—as opposed to the more abstract formulations of the story of Lonoikamakahiki and the Moikeha cycle—developed in the latter eighteenth to early nineteenth century. Hawaiian ethnologists are fairly agreed that such a story is not part of the ancient mythical corpus. The first versions we have of it date from the earlier nineteenth century (e.g., Freycinet 1978:73n; Bingham 1847:32; Ellis 1828:119; Kotzebue 1830 v.2:161–165; Bryon 1826:192). The myth, then, is not the charter of the Makahiki ceremony so much as it is the explication of Cook's advent and integration in the ceremony.

[9] On the comparison between the treatment afforded Europeans by Kamehameha and rival chiefs, see the accounts of Meares (1790), Portlock (1789), Dixon (1789) and Vancouver (1801).

[10] That this accumulative tendency, with its implication of an opposition in the economic relations of chiefs and people, was a response relative to the Hawaiian cultural order may be judged by comparison to Northwest Coast Indian chiefs under analogous conditions of trade—trade, indeed, with some of the same Europeans with whom the Hawaiians were dealing. Unlike the successive monopolization of guns, clothing and fine furnishings by the Hawaiian chiefs, their famous Indian counterparts—Maquinna, Kow, Cunneah—had as their main trade interest the distribution of goods (potlatching), to which end accumulation was a subordinate moment. It is reported that in 1803 Maquinna dispensed in one potlatch 200 muskets, 200 yards of cloth, 100 chemises, 100 looking glasses and seven barrels of gunpowder (Fisher 1977:18). In the same year, Kamehameha was amassing guns and ammunition, which he kept under his own control, for an invasion of Kauai.

[11] On the general history of the Hawaiian provisioning and sandalwood trade, see Morgan (1948), Bradley (1968), Kuykendall (1954), Howay (1930;1930-34) and Thrum (1905). Four specific measures of chiefly regulation: Dixon (1789:96-97,99, 104-106,111), Portlock (1789:154-157); Boit (Journal:15 October 1795); Broughton 1804; Anonymous (*Solid Men of Boston*); Howay (1937:26), Townsend (1888:61), Cleveland (n.d.), Lisiansky (1814:102-104), Ross (1849:36), Franchère (1969:60-61), Cox (1832:45,51), Corney (1896:*passim*), Hill (1937:366), Kotzebue (1821 v.1:293,313-314) and Wyllie (1856), among others.

[12] After Kamehameha had acceded to Vancouver's demand that he violate the Makahiki tabu, Vancouver unselfconsciously reports: "On my saying that this resolution made me very happy, and met my hearty concurrence, he replied, that I had treated him unkindly in suspecting that his friendship was abated, for that it remained unshaken, his future conduct would demonstrate; but that he considered himself to be the last person in his dominions who ought to violate the established laws, and the regulations of the country which he governed" (Vancouver 1801 v.5:9-10).

[13] A few pages later, as also in his personal journal, King tells of a woman who got a "terrible beating" on board the *Resolution* for eating the wrong type of banana; and a few sentences later in his journal he says "we saw no instances of the ill treatment of the Women" (*in* Beaglehole 1967:624).

[14] A number of excellent analyses have been made of the "cultural revolution" of 1819, respectively highlighting one or another precipitating condition: Davenport (1969), Webb (1965), Levin (1968), Fischer (1970) and Daws (1968b:53-60), among others. My own aim here is not to add another "causative" explanation, but to insert the event in a coherent structural-historical process—or at least to suggest this could be done, since only certain dimensions of the process are discussed here.

[15] The full extent of this disproportion, however, has to be judged from the mid-nineteenth century documents of the Lands Commission in the Archives of Hawaii. A later publication will document the distribution of land among various chiefs from 1795-1848.

[16] Among the descriptions of the events of the tabu abolition, see Thurston (1882:26-28), Dibble (1909:120ff), Alexander (1917), Remy (1861:133ff), R. Freycinet (1927) and L. Freycinet (1978). An important Hawaiian account, written by a Lahainaluna student in 1842 from information given by the old people, is deposited in the Bishop Museum (Lahainaluna [Anonymous]).

[17] Golovnin goes on to say that, in his experience, the women on no account break any of the prohibitions imposed on them. His compatriot Kotzebue, however, had two years earlier seen the corpse of a woman in Honolulu harbor, killed, the Russians were informed, for having entered a men's eating house while drunk. But besides hearsay about the women's transgressions, of which the Russians got other examples also in 1816, Kotzebue himself was at least once invited by "several ladies" to share a meal of dog they were preparing. He refused, presumably because the fare was not to his taste (*in* Kotzebue 1821 v.2:202; cf. Chamisso in the same volume, pp. 249-250).

[18] According to this tradition, the common people of the Hamakua and Waimea divisions—backcountry areas of Hawaii Island—resisted the *'ai noa* 'free eating'. "They followed the example of Kekuaokalani. They killed two free-eaters from Kona at Mahiki, and took their bones to Kaawaloa and offered them to Kekuaokalani" (Lahainaluna [Anonymous]).

¹⁹ Descriptions of this famous battle of Kuamoo indicate that Kekuaokalani was outgunned, if not outmanned. In the 1818–1819 account books of the American trader William French (HHS Archives; cf. Alexander 1904), King Kamehameha is debited with $8000 in guns, powder and shot in March, 1819; Liholiho in May also received 34 casks of gunpowder, 80 muskets, besides ball and flint. In these accounts, covering less than two years, Kamehameha and his chiefs parted with $61,000 in sandalwood. The account of Kaahumanu's collateral brother Boki amounted to $25,078, including three joint notes he assumed: one for the brig *Neo,* one for Kamehameha and one for (Billy Pitt) Kalaimoku.

References

ABBREVIATIONS

A.B.C.F.M.—American Board of Commissioners for Foreign Missions
AH   —Archives of Hawaii
BM   —British Museum
HEN   —Hawaiian Ethnographic Notes, Bishop Museum Library
HHS   —Hawaiian Historical Society
HMCS   —Hawaiian Mission Children's Society
PRO   —Public Records Office, London

A.B.C.F.M. Missionaries
  1821   Journal of the Missionaries. *Missionary Herald* 17:113–121.
Alexander, W. D.
  1904   Early Trading in Hawaii. *HHS Papers* 11:22–24.
  1917   Overthrow of the ancient tabu system in the Hawaiian Islands. *HHS, 25th Annual Report:* 37–45.
Anonymous
  Ms. Solid Men of Boston. Manuscript in the Bancroft Library, University of California, Berkeley.
Barrère, Dorothy, and Marshall Sahlins
  1979   Tahitians in the Early History of Hawaiian Christianity: The Journal of Toketa. *Hawaiian Journal of History* 13:19–35.
Beaglehole, John (ed.)
  1967   *The Journals of Captain James Cook on his Voyages of Discovery, III: The Voyage of the* Resolution *and* Discovery *1776–1780.* Parts One and Two. Cambridge: Cambridge University Press (for the Hakluyt Society).
Beckwith, Martha
  1919   The Hawaiian Romance of Laieikawai by S. N. Haleole. *Bureau of American Ethnology Report* 33:285–366. Washington: Government Printing Office.
  1970   *Hawaiian Mythology.* Honolulu: University of Hawaii Press.
  1972   *The Kumulipo: A Hawaiian Creation Chant.* Honolulu: University of Hawaii Press.
Bell, Edward
  1929–1930   Log of the *Chatham. Honolulu Mercury* I(4):7–26; I(5):55–69; I(6):76–96; II(1):80–91; II(2):119–129.
Best, Elsdon
  1923   Maori Personifications. *Journal of the Polynesian Society* 32:53–69, 103–120.
  1924   *Maori Religion and Mythology.* Dominion Museum Bulletin 10. Wellington: Government Printer.

Bingham, Hiram
1847 *Residence of Twenty-one Years in the Sandwich Islands.* New York: Praeger. (Reprint of the third, revised edition of 1855.)
Boit, John R.
Ms. The Journal of a Voyage Round the Globe [The *Union,* in Hawaii 1795]. Photostat of the second volume in HMCS. (Original in Massachusetts Historical Society.)
Bourdieu, Pierre
1977 *Outline of a Theory of Practice.* Translated by Richard Nice. Cambridge: Cambridge University Press.
Bradley, Harold Whitman
1968 *The American Frontier in Hawaii.* Gloucester, Mass.: Peter Smith. (Reissue of 1943 edition.)
Braudel, Fernand
1958 Histoire et sciences sociales: la longue durée. *Annales: Économies, Sociétés, Civilisations* 13:725–753.
Broughton, William Robert
1804 *A Voyage of Discovery to the North Pacific Ocean . . . in the Years 1795, 1796, 1797, 1798.* London: Cadell and Davies.
Burney, Lt. James
Ms. Journal of Lieutenant James Burney with Captain Ja^S Cook, 1776–1780. BM Add. MS 8955.
Byron, Captain The Right Honorable Lord [George Anson]
1826 *Voyage of the H.M.S. Blonde to the Sandwich Islands, in the Years 1824–1825.* London: Murray.
Campbell, Archibald
1819 *A Voyage Round the World.* New York: Broderick and Ritter.
Chamberlain, Levi
Ms. Journals I-XXIV, 11 November 1822–23 December 1843. Typescript in Bishop Museum Library.
Clerke, Captain James
Ms. Log and Proceedings of the *Discovery,* 10 1776–17 May 1778. AH: Cook Collection (photostat copy of PRO Adm 55/22).
Cleveland, Richard J.
n.d. *In the Forecastle; or, Twenty-five Years a Sailor.* New York: Manhattan Publishing Co.
Colnett, James
Ms. The Journal of James Colnett aboard the *Prince of Wales* and *Princess Royal* from 16 October 1786 to 7 November 1788. AH: Cook Collection (copy of original in PRO, London).
Ms. Journal of James Colnett of the *Argonaut,* March 29, 1791-April 18, 1791. AH: Cook Collection (copy of original in PRO, London).
Cook, Captain James, and Captain James King
1784 *A Voyage to the Pacific Ocean . . . in His Majesty's Ships* Resolution *and* Discovery. 3 vols. Dublin: H. Camberlaine et al.
Corney, Peter
1896 *Voyages in the Northern Pacific.* Honolulu: Thrum.
Cox, Ross
1832 *Adventures on the Columbia River.* New York: Harper.
Davenport, William
1969 The Hawaiian "Cultural Revolution": Some Economic and Political Considerations. *American Anthropologist* 71:1–20.

Daws, Gavan
1968a Kealakekua Bay Revisited: A Note on the Death of Captain Cook. *Journal of Pacific History* III:21-23.
1968b *Shoal of Time*. New York: Macmillan.
Dibble, Sheldon
1909 *A History of the Sandwich Islands*. Honolulu: Thrum. (A reissue of the 1843 work.)
Dixon, George
1789 *A Voyage Round the World Performed in 1785, 1786, 1787, and 1788*. London: Goulding.
Dumézil, Georges
1949 *L'Heritage Indo-européen à Rome*. 4th edition. Paris: Gallimard.
1970 *Archaic Roman Religion*. 2 vols. Chicago: University of Chicago Press.
Edgar, Thomas
Ms. A Journal of a Voyage undertaken to the South Seas. BM Add. MS 37528.
Ellis, William (surgeon)
1782 *An Authentic Narrative of a Voyage Performed by Captain Cook*. 2 vols. London: Robinson et al.
Ellis, William (missionary)
1828 *Narrative of a Tour Through Hawaii, or Owhyhee*. 4th edition. London: Fisher and Jackson.
Emerson, Nathaniel B.
1915 *Pele and Hiiaka: A Myth from Hawaii*. Honolulu: Honolulu Star Bulletin.
Fischer, J. L.
1970 Political Factors in the Overthrow of the Hawaiian Taboo System. *Acta Ethnographica Academiae Scientiarum Hungaricae* 19:161-167.
Fisher, Robin
1977 *Contact and Conflict: Indian-European Relations in British Columbia, 1774–1890*. Vancouver: University of British Columbia Press.
Fleurieu, C. P. Claret
1801 *A Voyage Round the World Performed During the Years 1790, 1791, and 1792, by Etienne Marchand*. Vol. I. London: Longman and Rees.
Fornander, Abraham
1916-19 *Fornander Collection of Hawaiian Antiquities and Folk-lore*. Translation edited by Thos. G. Thrum. Memoirs of the Bernice Pauahi Bishop Museum, Vols. IV-VI.
1969 *An Account of the Polynesian Race*. (Three volumes in one.) Rutland and Tokyo: Charles E. Tuttle. (First published in 1878-1885.)
Franchère, Gabriel
1969 *Journal of a Voyage on the Northwest Coast of North America During the Years 1811, 1812, 1813, and 1814*. Translated by Wessie Tipping Lamb. Toronto: The Champlain Society. (First published 1820.)
French, William
Ms. Account book, said to be of William French, 1818-1819. HHS Library.
Freycinet, Louis Claude de Saulses de
1978 *Hawaii in 1819: A Narrative Account*. Translated by Ella Wiswell from his *Voyage autour du monde pendant les années 1817-1829*, Paris, 1827-1839. Edited by Marion Kelly. Honolulu: Bishop Museum, Pacific Anthropological Records, 26.
Freycinet, Rose Marie (Pinon) de Saulses de
1927 *Compagne de L'Uranie (1917-1820): Journal de Madame Rose de Saulses de Freycinet*. Paris: Société d'Editions Géographiques, Maritimes et Coloniales.

Gilbert, George
  Ms. Journal of George Gilbert (with Cook). BM Add. MS 38530.
Gill, Rev. William Wyatt
  1876 *Myths and Songs from the South Pacific.* London: King.
Golovnin, V. M.
  1979 *Around the World on the Kamchatka, 1817–1819.* Translated by Ella Wiswell. Honolulu: Hawaiian Historical Society and University of Hawaii Press.
Grey, Sir George
  1956 *Polynesian Mythology.* Auckland: Whitcombe and Tombs.
Hammett, Charles H.
  Ms. Journal of Charles H. Hammett Two Years' Stay in the Sandwich Islands, May 6, 1823-June 9, 1825. Copy in HMCS Library, Honolulu. (Original in Baker Library, Harvard University.)
Handy, E. S. Craighill
  n.d. Cultural Revolution in Hawaii. Honolulu: Institute of Pacific Relations.
  1923 *The Native Culture in the Marquesas.* Bernice P. Bishop Museum Bulletin 9.
Handy, E. S. Craighill, and Mary Kawena Pukui
  1972 *The Polynesian Family System in Ka-'u, Hawai'i.* Rutland and Tokyo: Charles E. Tuttle.
Hill, Samuel
  1937 Voyage of the Ophelia. Edited by James W. Snyder, Jr. *The New England Quarterly* 10:355–380.
Hocart, A. M.
  1927 *Kingship.* London: Oxford University Press.
  1933 *The Progress of Man.* London: Methuen.
Howay, Frederic William
  1930 Early Relations Between the Hawaiian Islands and the Northwest Coast. In *The Hawaiian Islands . . . Captain Cook Sesquicentennial Celebration,* edited by Albert P. Taylor and Ralph S. Kuykendall. Honolulu: AH Publication No. 5, pp. 11–21.
  1930–34 A List of Trading Vessels in the Maritime Fur Trade, 1795 . . . to . . . 1825. *The Transactions of the Royal Society of Canada,* Third Series, Section 2, 24:111–134; 25:117–149; 26:43–86; 27:119–147; 28:11–49.
  1937 The "Caroline" and the "Hancock" at Hawaii in 1799. *HHS Annual Report for 1936,* 45:25–29.
Hubert, Henri, and Marcel Mauss
  1964 *Sacrifice: Its Nature and Function.* Translated by W. D. Halls. Chicago: University of Chicago Press.
Hunnewell, James
  Ms. Letters and Papers. Hunnewell Collection: Baker Library, Harvard University.
  1864 Letter from James Hunnewell, Boston, 24 June 1863. *The Friend,* January 1864: 5.
I'i, John Papa
  1959 *Fragments of Hawaiian History.* Translated by Mary Kawena Pukui. Honolulu: Bishop Museum Press.
Irving, Washington
  1836 *Astoria or Anecdotes of an Enterprise beyond the Rocky Mountains.* 2 vols. Philadelphia: Carey, Lea and Blanchard.
Iselin, Isaac
  n.d. *Journal of a Trading Voyage Around the World, 1805–1808.* New York: McIlroy and Emmet.
Jakobson, Roman
  1961 *Selected Writings I.* The Hague: Mouton.

Johansen, J. Prytz
1954 *The Maori and His Religion.* Copenhagen: Munksgaard.
Kamakau, Samuel M.
Ms. Na Mo'olelo Hawaii. Ms. in the Bishop Museum, Honolulu.
1865 The Travels to Noted Places: Demigods and the Ancient Chiefs from Hawaii to Niihau. Translated by Mary K. Pukui from *Ka Nupepa Kuokoa,* 15 June 1865. HEN II:697–700.
1961 *Ruling Chiefs of Hawaii.* Honolulu: Kamehameha Schools Press.
1964 *Ka Po'e Kahiko: The People of Old.* Translated by Mary Kawena Pukui; edited by Dorothy B. Barrère. Honolulu: Bishop Museum Press.
1976 *The Works of the People of Old: Na Hana a ka Po'e Kahiko.* Translated by Mary Kawena Pukui; edited by Dorothy B. Barrère. Honolulu: Bishop Museum Press.
Kant, Immanuel
1965 *Critique of Pure Reason.* Translated by Norman Kemp Smith. New York: St. Martin's Press.
Kekoa, E.
1865 Birth Rites of Hawaiian Children in Ancient Times. Translated from *Kuokoa* (newspaper) by T. Thrum. Bishop Museum Library: Thrum Collection 23.
Kelly, Marion
1967 Some Problems with Early Descriptions of Hawaiian Culture. In *Polynesian Culture History: Essays in Honor of Kenneth P. Emory,* edited by Genevieve A. Highland et al. Honolulu: Bishop Museum Press, Bernice P. Bishop Museum Special Publication 56.
Kepelino, Z.
1932 *Kepelino's Traditions of Hawaii.* Edited by Martha Beckwith. Bernice P. Bishop Museum Bulletin 95.
1977 Kepelino's "Hawaiian Collection": His *Hooiliili Havaii,* Pepa I, 1858. Translated by Bacil F. Kirtley and Esther T. Mookini. *Hawaiian Journal of History* 11:39–68.
King, Lt. James
Ms. Log and Proceedings of the *Resolution,* 12 February 1776–1 February 1778. PRO Adm. 55/116.
Kotzebue, Otto von
1821 *A Voyage of Discovery into the South Sea . . . in the Years 1815–1818.* 3 vols. London: Longman et al.
1830 *A New Voyage Round the World.* 2 vols. London: Colburn and Bentley.
Kroeber, A. L.
1948 *Anthropology.* Rev. ed. New York: Harcourt, Brace.
Kuykendall, Ralph S.
1968 *The Hawaiian Kingdom. Vol. 1: 1778–1854.* Honolulu: University of Hawaii Press.
Lahainaluna [Anonymous]
Ms. Ka 'ainoa—Free Eating—from Earliest Times until its Proclamation," 30 January, 1842; by a student of the Seminary. Translated by D. Barrère. Lahainaluna Paper 4, Bishop Museum Library.
Law, John
Ms. Journal of John Law, Surgeon (with Cook), 1779. BM Add. MS 37327.
Lévi-Strauss, Claude
1966 *The Savage Mind.* Chicago: University of Chicago Press.
Levin, Stephanie Seto
1968 The Overthrow of the *Kapu* System in Hawaii. *Journal of the Polynesian Society* 77:402–430.

Lisiansky, Urey
   1814   *A Voyage Around the World in the Years, 1803, 1804, 1805, and 1806.* London: Booth.
Makemson, Maud Worcestor
   1939–1939   Hawaiian Astronomical Concepts. *American Anthropologist* 40:370–383; 41:589–596.
   1941   *The Morning Star Rises.* New Haven: Yale University Press.
Malo, David
   1951   *Hawaiian Antiquities.* Second edition. Translated by Dr. Nathaniel B. Emerson. Honolulu: Bishop Museum Press.
Manby, Thomas
   1929   Journal of Vancouver's Voyage to the Pacific Ocean. *Honolulu Mercury* I(1): 11–15; I(2):33–45; I(3):39–55.
Martin, John, ed.
   1817   *An Account of the Natives of the Tonga Islands . . . Compiled and Arranged from the Extensive Communications of Mr. William Mariner.* 2 vols. London: Murray.
Mathison, Gilbert Farquhar
   1825   *Narrative of a Visit to Brazil, Chile, Peru and the Sandwich Islands During the Years 1821 and 1822.* London: Knight.
Meares, John
   1790   *Voyages Made in the Years 1788 and 1789, from China to the Northwest Coast of America, to which are Prefixed an Introductory Narrative of a Voyage Performed in 1786, from Bengal, in the Ship Nootka.* London: Logographic Press.
Menzies, Archibald
   Ms.   Archibald Menzies' Journal of Vancouver's Voyage. BM Add. MS 32641.
Morgan, Theodore
   1948   *Hawaii: A Century of Economic Change 1778–1876.* Cambridge, Mass.: Harvard University Press.
Nicol, John
   1822   *The Life and Adventures of John Nicol, Mariner.* Edinburgh: William Blackwood.
Percy, Walker
   1958   Symbol, Consciousness and Intersubjectivity. *The Journal of Philosophy* 55: 631–641.
Portlock, Nathaniel
   1789   *A Voyage around the World . . . in 1785, 1786, 1787, and 1788.* London: Stockdale.
Pouillon, Jean
   1977   Plus c'est la même chose, plus ça change. *Nouvelle Revue de Psychanalyse* 15:203–211.
Puget, Lt. Peter
   Ms.   Fragments of Journals 1792–1794. BM Add. MS 17546–17548.
   Ms.   A Log of the Proceedings of His Majesty's Armed Tender *Chatham,* 1793–1794. PRO Adm. 55/17.
Pukui, Mary Kawena, and Samuel H. Elbert
   1965   *Hawaiian-English Dictionary.* 3rd edition. Honolulu: University of Hawaii Press.
Pukui, Mary Kawena, E. W. Haertig and Catherine A. Lee
   1972   *Nana i ke Kumu (Look to the Source).* Volume I. Honolulu: Hui Hanai.
Remy, Jules
   1861   *Ka Mooolelo Hawaii (Histoire Havaiienne).* Paris: Clave. (A French translation and Hawaiian text of the Lahainaluna Students *Mo'o'olelo* of 1838.)

Reynolds, Stephen
   Ms. Journal of Stephen Reynolds, November 1823–December 1843. Microfilm copy, HMCS Library, Honolulu. (Original in Peabody Museum, Salem.)
Rickman, Lt. John (attributed)
   1781 *Journal of Captain Cook's Last Voyage to the Pacific.* London: E. Newberry.
Riou, Edward
   Ms. A Logg of the Proceedings of his Majesty's Sloop *Discovery,* 1778–1779. PRO Adm. 51/4529.
Ross, Alexander
   1849 *Adventures of the First Settlers on the Oregon or Columbia River.* London: Smith, Elder.
Sahlins, Marshall
   1977 The State of the Art in Social/Cultural Anthropology: Search for an Object. In *Perspectives on Anthropology 1976,* edited by Anthony F. C. Wallace et al. American Anthropological Association Special Publication, 10.
   1979 L'apothéose du captaine Cook. In *La fonction symbolique,* edited by Michel Izard and Pierre Smith. Paris: Gallimard.
Salmond, Anne
   1978 Te ao tawhito: A Semantic Approach to the Traditional Maori Cosmos. *Journal of the Polynesian Society* 87:5–28.
Saussure, Ferdinand de
   1966 *Course in General Linguistics.* New York: McGraw-Hill. (First French edition 1915; English translation by Wade Baskin.)
Shaler, William
   1808 Journal of a Voyage Between China and the North-western Coast of America Made in 1804. *American Register* 3:137–175.
Smith, Jean
   1974–1975 Tapu Removal in Maori Religion. *Journal of the Polynesian Society* 83: 9–42; 84:43–58; 59–96.
Taylor, Richard
   1870 *Te ika a Maori or New Zealand and its Inhabitants.* Second edition. London: Macintosh.
Thrum, Thomas G.
   1905 The Sandalwood Trade of Early Hawaii. *Hawaiian Annual* 31:43–74.
   1923 *More Hawaiian Folk Tales.* Chicago: McClurg.
Thurston, Lucy G.
   1882 *Life and Times of Mrs. Lucy G. Thurston.* Ann Arbor: Andrews.
Townsend, Ebenezer, Jr.
   1888 The Diary of Mr. Ebenezer Townsend, Jr. *Papers of the New Haven Colony Historical Society* 4:1–115.
Turnbull, John
   1805 *A Voyage Round the World in the Years 1800, 1801, 1802, 1803, and 1804.* . . . 3 vols. London: Richard Phillips.
Tyerman, Daniel, and George Bennet
   1831 *Journal of Voyages and Travels.* Vol. 1. London: Westley and Davis.
Valeri, Valerio
   n.d. *Hai Kanaka: le chef Hawaiien et son sacrifice.* Cambridge: Cambridge University Press (in press).
Vancouver, Captain George
   1801 *A Voyage of Discovery to the North Pacific Ocean . . . in the Years 1790, 1791, 1792, 1793, 1794 and 1795.* New Edition, 5 vols. London: John Stockdale.

Wagner, Roy
  1975   *The Invention of Culture.* Englewood Cliffs: Prentice-Hall.
Webb, M. C.
  1965   The Abolition of the Taboo System in Hawaii. *Journal of the Polynesian Society* 74:21–39.
Westervelt, W. D.
  1923   *Hawaiian Historical Legends.* New York: Revell.
White, John
  1887–1890   *Ancient History of the Maori, His Mythology and Traditions.* 6 vols. Wellington: Government Printer.
Whitman, John B.
  Ms.   Account of the Sandwich Islands 1813–1815. Microfilm copy in HMCS of original in Peabody Museum, Salem.
Wyllie, Robert C.
  1856   *Supplement to the Report of the Minister of Foreign Relations to the Legislature in 1856.* Honolulu: Government Printer.
Zimmermann, Heinrich
  1930   *Zimmermann's Captain Cook: An Account of the Third Voyage of Captain Cook around the World, 1776–1780.* Translated from the Mannheim edition of 1781 by Elsa Michaelis and Cecil French. Edited by F. W. Howay. Toronto: Ryerson Press.